Through the Perilous Night
Khobar Bombing Survivors Remember

Paul Sherbo

REMEMBERING THE LIVES
Of those lost in the terrorist attack on
Khobar Towers on June 25, 1996.

We Shall Never Forget

Christopher J. Adams, Massapequa Park, New York

Daniel B. Cafourek, Watertown, South Dakota

Millard D. Campbell, Angelton, Texas

Earl F. Carrette Jr., Sellersburg, Indiana

Patrick Feenig, Greendale, Wisconsin

Leland T. Haun, Clovis, California

Michael G. Heiser, Palm Coast, Florida

Kevin J. Johnson, Shreveport, Louisiana

Ronald L. King, Battlecreek, Michigan

Kendall K.J. Kitson, Yukon, Oklahoma

Christopher Lester, Pineville, West Virginia

Brian W. McVeigh, DeBary, Florida

Brent E. Marthaler, Cambridge, Minnesota

Peter J. Morgera, Stratham, New Hampshire

Thanh V. Nguyen, Panama City, Florida

Joseph E. Rimkus, Niceville, Florida

Jeremy A. Taylor, Rose Hill, Kansas

Justin R. Wood, Modesto, California

Joshua E. Woody, Corning, California

Through the Perilous Night:
Khobar Bombing Survivors Remember
Copyright © 2021 by Paul Sherbo
First Edition printed 2021
All rights reserved.

This is a non-fiction title. It is a compilation of stories from survivors of the terrorist bombing of Khobar Towers in Dhahran, Saudi Arabia, June 25, 1996, and includes personal interviews with surviving U.S. Military members, with quotations from witness testimony as transcribed into records investigating, and/or litigating, the attack. We assume no responsibility for errors or inconsistencies herein.

ISBN-13: 978-1-7323764-1-0

Library of Congress Control Number:
2020942905

Managing Editor: Dari Bradley
Assistant Editor: Sydney Schermerhorn
Technical Advisor: Nelson Ottenhausen
Cover Photo: Jim Lamb, Jim Lamb Photography
Cover Design & Graphics: Bruce Gardner
Cover Base Photo: U.S. Department of Defense

Published by Patriot Media Incorporated
Publishing America's Patriots
P.O. Box 5414
Niceville, FL 32578
United States of America
patriotmediainc.com

No part of this book may be reproduced or transmitted in any form or by any means, electronic or mechanical, including photocopying, recording or information storage and retrieval systems without the expressed written approval of the author with the exception of a reviewer who may quote brief passages in a review printed by a newspaper, magazine, journal or online blog. The appearance of the U.S. Department of Defense (DoD) visual information does not imply or constitute DoD endorsement.

Unless otherwise stated, photographs are credited to the U.S. Air Force.

DEDICATION

To the fallen, the wounded, and the veterans of the 1996 terrorist attack and of the struggles of the survivors.

"You may have to fight a battle more than once to win it."
— Margaret Thatcher

ACKNOWLEDGEMENTS

No one can tell the story of an ordeal like this without being humbled by the endurance of those who suffered through it and who endure it still. Because I recognize that no one's trial under fire is more or less important than the others, I list here those I interviewed in alphabetical order. I salute them all.

Bridget Brooks

Doug Cochran

Scott Coleman

Terry Michael Dunn Jr.

Trena Frazier-Schmidt

John Gaydos

Angel Hebert-Marsh

Dusty Huntley

Jessica (Kowalczyk) Bradshaw

Larry Oliver

Leighton Reid

William Schooley

Michael Willis

Scott Wolff

Selena Zuhoski

PREFACE

The most common trait among the people interviewed for this book is absolute lack of self-pity.

Many admit to the fear they felt when a terrorist bomb exploded next to the Khobar Towers compound in Saudi Arabia in June 1996. Many admit to initial disorientation that briefly sidelined them before they could begin to respond. More than a few admit to images and feelings that haunted them over the years.

In spite of all that, they have moved ahead and look back at the trauma as something that has forged them into who they are today.

One of them, Jessica Bradshaw, put it this way–echoing the words of many veterans throughout history:

> "It's not like I did this challenge and I survived. That's not it. It made me more humble as a person and more empathetic, especially since my dad was in Vietnam. I mean, I never got that. And I think I have a little piece of what he endured."

"Adversity introduces a man to himself."
— *Albert Einstein*

Through the Perilous Night

CHAPTER 1
Overture

It was one of the first shots in what would come to be known as the *Global War on Terror*.

On the late evening of June 25, 1996, a terrorist-made truck bomb exploded just outside of a Coalition Forces housing base in Saudi Arabia. Before the attack, few outside of the military had ever heard the name of the complex – Khobar Towers.

It was home to Coalition Forces assigned to establish and monitor Iraqi no-fly zones in accordance with U.N. Security Council resolutions.

Nineteen United States service members died. Scores of Coalition members from the U.S and other countries were injured.

The tragedy had, as many tragedies do, many heroes– people who ignored their own safety and injuries to save and assist the wounded. What had once been their homes turned into deadly jumbles of rubble that trapped and disoriented survivors and those with little time left.

Those who safely escaped from blasted and darkened buildings nevertheless charged back in to search for more survivors. Injured airmen waved off medical care, directing rescuers to others with more serious injuries.

Herein are but a few stories of the many who rose to the occasion. There are many more such stories, and far more than can fit in one narrative.

Many of the survivors ultimately came together in the Khobar Towers Bombing Survivors Association – more than 500 strong, bearing witness to one of a long train of terrorist attacks.

Over more than two decades, the Association has sought justice for those who were unfairly held accountable for the tragedy as well as accountability for those who ducked their responsibility.

Here is the story of the assault, as told by some of the Veterans of Khobar. There are hundreds of such stories. The ones in this account are not by any means the most important, the bravest or the best. But together they build a saga of ordinary men and women rising to meet extraordinary circumstances. It is also the story of survivors who continue to forge ahead.

CHAPTER 2
Anthem

The men and women who would face the opening salvo of terrorist attacks came together from across the American landscape.

Leighton Reid was born in 1954 and began his journey in the suburbs north of Detroit in St. Clair Shores.

His parents ran a pharmacy. In the days before 24-hour pharmacy chains, that meant long days, seven days a week, with occasional emergency calls from the hospital to fill prescriptions at two or three in the morning.

"I grew up in the drugstore, I wasn't born there, obviously, but damn near. I essentially raised myself as both parents were in the store from nine in the morning until eleven at night."

Reid's introduction to military life came from the husband of one of his two sisters, who married a soldier. He would spend his summers with them wherever they were stationed.

His last two years of high school were the late 60s, and the family worried about the growing prevalence of illegal drugs. When the Army posted his brother-in-law to Germany, he offered to take Reid along for his last two years of high school.

"Not a hard choice. Took me about a half a nanosecond."

He spent two years going to a Department of Defense (DoD) school off-base along with students from other English-speaking families, Americans and Canadians. He also bought his first car, a Volkswagen Beetle, for $50 and learned to fix it himself.

The DoD high school offered a "work study" program at the local Armed Forces Network (AFN) TV station on neighboring Ramstein Air Base. There he learned basic lighting, camera operations and the ins and outs of television and broadcast media. He occasionally was in front of the camera interviewing guests or – on a children's show – "dancing around in a bear costume."

Following high school, he married his high school sweetheart and moved back to Michigan. About that time, the draft was replaced by the lottery system, and he learned his number while watching the lottery numbers chosen on television. In the years leading up to his eligibility, his birth date ranked in the 300s. But not that year.

He was number 17.

"The Vietnam War was winding down but it was still going on. I was kind of bummed out, I had just got married and everything, I was going to college."

At a local auto show shortly afterward, he talked with an Air Force recruiter who, in a story familiar to many Veterans, "guaranteed" him work in radio and TV production.

"Yeah it was a guaranteed job all right. There was a television set in the back seat of an F-4 fighter connected to the aircraft's radar."

After nine months of electronics training at Lowry Air Force Base in Denver, Reid went to MacDill Air Force Base in Florida.

When the Air Force studied the disastrous effects of a chemical attack on Israel in the 1973 Arab-Israeli War, he was reassigned to the disaster preparedness program.

Reid served in West Berlin during the Cold War, living in an apartment from which he could see over the wall into Communist East Berlin.

When he completed several tours, including Korea, the disaster preparedness program was absorbed into the Air Base Operability Program, aimed at making air bases self-sufficient in protecting themselves while flying missions.

***

Larry Oliver was raised in Vernon, Connecticut, the son of a real estate agent and a stay-at home mother. He attended a technical high school in the nearby town of Manchester, where he studied to be an electrician and graduated in 1990 in a class of about 125.

Oliver remembers fishing a lot as he grew up, catching mostly trout at first and later hooking bass. He preferred bass because "they're a lot more fun."

"As I got older I got into target shooting and pursued that for a while," he recalls, starting with a .22 rifle.

Following high school, Oliver worked as an electrician until March 1993. Then he followed up on an agreement with a childhood friend.

"We always had a deal where if one of us joined the military, the other would too," he said. "One day we said, screw it, let's do it. And we did."

He chose the Air Force Security Police because…

"I think it had to do with the fact that I like to shoot."

And because he found a special talent when he had to help "de-escalate situations."

"I always liked being a peacemaker."

After basic training and Security Police schools, Oliver served at Royal Air Force Base Alconbury in England and later at Eglin Air Force Base in Florida. He deployed to the Khobar Towers in 1996.

***

William Schooley's life began in 1961 in Albuquerque New Mexico.

"I had several family members who were ex-military, including my father who was a Marine Corps officer, another uncle who was also a Marine and fought throughout the Pacific. Also, I had an uncle who was a pilot in WWII and eventually flew the SR-71.

But the person who had the biggest impact was an uncle who was also a WWII pilot and test pilot, Colonel 'Lanky' Harrison, who often took me flying in his hot air balloon.

In fact, one of strongest memories was years later, at a family funeral, Lanky came up to me. I was wearing my Dress Blues. He said, 'I see you have *earned* the finest suit of clothes a man can own!' Possibly the best complement I have ever received!"

Schooley enlisted in the Air Force as a Munitions Systems Specialist, otherwise known as an Ammo Troop.

"It is a great thing when you find the job you are meant for."

He met and married Missy, who was also a Munitions Specialist, in 1995. While stationed at Kirtland Air Force Base in New Mexico, he got the orders that would put him on the path to King Abdul Aziz Air Base at Dhahran and the Khobar Towers.

***

Trena (Frazier) Schmidt was born in September 1969, the daughter of Donnie Frazier, a school bus driver and school district maintenance man, and Judy Donaldson, a textile worker. Describing herself as a *"tomboy,"* Schmidt grew up on a farm near Savannah, Tennessee, raising corn, soybeans, cattle, horses, goats and chickens, and enjoying dirt biking, fishing and hunting.

She graduated from high school in 1987 and didn't waste any time moving on from there.

"I graduated on a Friday and left Monday morning for the Air Force. I was 17 years old."

Her parents had to sign permission for her to enlist due to her age.

From boot camp at San Antonio, Texas, she went to Lowry Air Force Base near Denver, Colorado, to train in the field of Aircraft Armament Weapons Loader. Assignments to Kunsan Air Base in Korea and MacDill Air Force Base in Florida followed.

Over the course of her career, Schmidt retrained into the field of Aircraft Structural Maintenance and eventually into environmental, safety and occupational health.

Along the way, Schmidt was promoted to E4 ahead of her peers. She was airman of the quarter numerous times and non-commissioned officer of the year while stationed at Kirtland Air Force Base in New Mexico.

She also earned her bachelor's degree in Environmental Science while at Kirtland. At MacDill, she was awarded a one and a half hour ride in an F-16D due to her superior performance.

Schmidt did all this at a time when women were not prominent in the military, particularly in her field.

"Most of the time I was one of the few females around. I was the only female in my tech school class."

From Pope Air Force Base in North Carolina, Schmidt deployed to Saudi Arabia and Khobar Towers for a month in October 1994. This was followed by a three-month deployment to Kuwait and, in April 1996, back to Khobar.

At the time, she was a Staff Sergeant (E5).

***

Angel (Hebert) Marsh, daughter of Henry and Minnie Hebert, was born in November of 1973 in Lafayette, Louisiana. Her father worked in oilfields as a drilling superintendent. Her mother was a busy homemaker – Marsh was the last of eight children.

When Marsh was in the seventh grade the family moved to Mandeville, near New Orleans, with her father's job. In school, Marsh played softball and was a member of the high school band. In the band, musical instruments were not her forte – instead, "I twirled a rifle."

Marsh tried college for about two years but "it turns out I like to go out more than I like to go to class."

She worked for Office Depot for a while, then just before turning 21 she went to see an Air Force recruiter. January 1995 found her in basic training. After additional schooling as a fuels specialist, her first duty station was Barksdale Air Force Base near Shreveport: "I didn't even know there was a base there."

From Barksdale, Marsh deployed to Khobar as an Airman First Class (E3).

***

Through the Perilous Night

Scott Wolff was born in 1958 in northern Wisconsin. His father, Walter, was a World War II Veteran and paper mill employee. His mother, Betty, worked in a shoe factory.

Wolff remembers a childhood of hunting, fishing and camping, "mostly with my Dad and Mom" and a cousin, Jim Wolff, who was about the same age.

He graduated from high school in 1978 and went into the Air Force just 20 days after graduation.

"I had an uncle that was in the Air Force and I was kind of interested in jet engines. So I went in the Air Force and became a jet engine mechanic."

After boot camp in San Antonio came technical school at Chanute Air Force Base in Illinois. A career with duty in South Carolina, New Mexico, Spain and Korea, among other places, followed.

Over the years, Wolff was sent various places on temporary duty. From Shaw Air Force Base in South Carolina, the Air Force sent him to Saudi Arabia in the spring of 1996. By that time, he was a master sergeant (E7).

***

Another self-described *tomboy*, **Jessica (Kowalczyk) Bradshaw**, was born in 1973, in Erie, Pennsylvania. Her father, Fred, worked for General Electric, and her mother, Barb, was a homemaker.

Growing up, Bradshaw was always into sports- basketball, volleyball and softball.

Bradshaw decided to join the service after graduating from high school in 1991. Her father, an Army Veteran of Vietnam, tried to talk her out of it.

"He said 'I'll give you a thousand dollars not to join' because he had a bad experience being in Vietnam."

She nonetheless entered the Air Force in December 1991, went into Air Base Ground Defense training, had "awesome" duty at Upper Hayford Air Base, England, plus duty in Turkey, Nevada and Honduras.

In 1995 and 96 she was at Holloman Air Force Base. She attended Traffic Investigation School in Texas in 1995. Orders to go to Saudi Arabia came about after an incident that occurred when her flight commander assigned her to flight line duty, instead of her regular duties as a desk sergeant or a patrolman.

A major accident had happened on base. Because of her assignment to flight line duty, it took her 40 minutes to get to the scene. This was because she had to leave the flight line, turn in an M-16, draw a Beretta, and get to the accident.

Her flight commander "was talked to" about the late response to investigate the accident. Next thing Bradshaw knew, she had orders to the desert despite initially having been at the bottom of the deployment list.

She arrived at Khobar Towers in May 1996.

***

Doug Cochran was born in 1955, and grew up in Maryland. He is the oldest of five children, with three brothers and a sister. He spent his early years near Rockville, and after age 10 lived near what is now Columbia.

The area surrounding Cochran's neighborhood was semi-rural and loaded with a lot of children near his age. He played sports, mostly baseball. In scouting, he attained the rare distinction of the rank of Eagle Scout.

At a career day for Eagle Scouts, Cochran chose the Air Force offer of a tour to visit Andrews Air Force Base.

"When I saw the F-4 fighter jet, I thought then and there I wanted to join the Air Force. Not a popular thing at the time to join the military– Vietnam War was still underway."

Following Boy Scouts, Cochran joined Explorer scouts and flew a couple of times with an Aviation Explorer Post.

"Really started to get the flying bug now."

Cochran met his future wife, Resa, on an Explorer canoe trip. They both attended Atholton High School and the University of Maryland in College Park, Cochran using a four-year Air Force ROTC scholarship. They married the year following college graduation.

Although he was selected as a pilot candidate, at the end of his college junior year, the Air Force took away the pilot slots. The Vietnam war over now and they were downsizing the pilot force.

"I elected to continue in the program and was selected to enter the Air Force as a second lieutenant in the Security Police. I graduated with a Law Enforcement degree."

His first assignment was at McGuire Air Force Base in New Jersey.

"While there I reapplied for Undergraduate Pilot Training at every opportunity and after two years I was selected."

Cochran graduated from the training in 1981, and was assigned at Laughlin Air Force Base in Texas as a T-38 instructor. In 1984, he was selected for F-15 training. A variety of assignments followed, including a year at Keflavik, Iceland, as assistant operations officer, then Air Command and Staff College at Maxwell Air Force Base in Alabama. In 1995, he was selected as Commander of the 58th Fighter Squadron at Eglin Air Force Base in Florida.

His squadron was scheduled to deploy to Dhahran from April to June 1996.

"The squadron had just returned from there 13 months prior, before my tenure, the night of departure, after briefing for the trip across the Atlantic, we were informed the tankers were on weather hold and cancelled for that night. We rolled to the next night and successfully launched 18 jets headed for Germany.

We went through the worst weather I've ever flown in, going across the Atlantic. Enroute we had several in-flight emergencies and ended up diverting eight to 10 jets to airports and bases in Canada and Scotland."

After about a week of various delays, the squadron finally arrived.

***

T. Michael "Mike" Dunn Jr. was born in Zanesville, Ohio, in 1973. His father Terry had just joined the Army, where, among other jobs, he worked as a tank mechanic and a cook. His mother Vicki tended to the home. Together the family spent four years at Fort Riley in Kansas.

The Dunns moved back to Zanesville, where Mike attended high school. He remembers himself there as "mostly a misfit" who "really enjoyed skateboarding."

His enlistment in the Air Force was not in his plans. But, as he recalls, "I was friends with the Air Force recruiter's son."

After boot camp, Dunn went to Biloxi where he attended technical school to become a ground radio communications specialist, "ground rat" for short. In 1992, he married his first wife. They had a daughter in 1995.

Following duty in New Mexico and Texas, Dunn was ready to finish his career in San Antonio. He was in the process of getting out when his unit, an intelligence squadron, got the word that the Air Force needed a ground radio specialist for duty in Saudi Arabia.

***

Michael Willis was born in Beaufort, North Carolina, in 1966. He is the son of Clyde Willis, a commercial fisherman, and Nancy Willis, a bank employee. Young Willis crewed on his father's boat, harvesting shrimps, crabs and oysters. He even took to the sea himself. Before graduating from East Carteret High School in 1985, he had his own boat in the fishing business.

Willis started college at North Carolina State University, but when money got tight he enlisted in the Air Force in 1987.

He attended basic and technical training at Lackland Air Force Base in San Antonio, Texas, and specialized in secure communications maintenance – basically the hardware side of anything that had to do with communications, including computers, telephones, radios and satellites.

From 1987 to 1993, Willis was stationed at Wright Patterson Air Force Base in Ohio. He married Shelly Baney from Huber Heights, Ohio, in 1991. He spent a year at Osan Air Base in Korea before going to Langley Air Force Base in Virginia in 1994. There he was assigned to an intelligence unit. The unit deployed to Khobar in 1994 and would spend three months at Khobar, six months stateside and then repeat the cycle for three years.

Willis described the time at Khobar as "routine." Days were taken up mostly by 12-hour shifts, followed by volleyball games or working out at the gym. At this time he was a staff sergeant.

"It was a tight knit unit. People knew their jobs, we knew each other."

Overall, Willis described the time as "a mundane existence."

"You had to figure out what day of the week it was part of the time."

On June 25, 1996, Willis was on his third tour of duty in three years. He had been in country for just a few days and wasn't scheduled to leave until early September.

"After finishing work one evening, I was riding in the bus around the perimeter and saw an old fuel truck parked next to one of the dorms. I remember thinking that would be a good place for someone to plant a bomb."

***

For Aeromedical Specialist **Benjamin Scott Coleman**, who goes by "Scott," Dhahran was his first deployment.

Coleman was an Airman First Class Aeromedical Specialist, also known as a Flight Medicine Tech. He was stationed at Little Rock Air Force Base when he got orders to the 61st Air Squadron, headed for that area of the world that many in the military refer to simply, but not so fondly, as "the sandbox."

"This was my first time ever outside the US, so I braced myself and hoped for the best. We rotated in on or about May 15th. The smell of Saudi is the first thing I noticed as we boarded the bus from the flight line. That odor was the smell of a sewage treatment plant. I had heard how miserable Khobar Towers was going to be but tried not to take too much stock in it."

***

Dusty Huntley was born in Kokomo, Indiana, in 1967, the son of Chrysler worker Donald Huntley and Delco Electronics employee Linda Huntley. His main activities growing up were baseball, archery, roller-skating and cars.

Huntley started his working years as a paper boy at age 11, progressing to McDonalds and then Sears by age 17. He graduated high school in 1986 and took a six-month delayed Air Force enlistment in January 1987. He married his wife Roberta in July 1987. They raised two sons.

The deployment to Khobar in 1996 was his first deployment. He was a staff sergeant fuel specialist. He remembers June 25 as —

"A typical evening and I was getting ready for work. I was the mid-shift supervisor. We were looking forward to the upcoming weekend as were promised some R&R at Bahrain."

***

Selena Zuhoski was born July 31, 1962, the only child of Bob and Linda Pytlik, in Albany, Georgia. When she was two, the family moved to Tampa, Florida, "and I consider that my hometown."

"It was an amazing childhood."

An only child, her parents both worked full time, and Dad also went to school.

"I spent a lot of time by myself growing up. I'd come home from school and I'd let myself into the house. I usually made dinner for my parents.

I developed, at a really young age, an interest in cooking. That has stayed with me throughout my whole life. When I joined the military, every place that I went to, throughout the world, one of the main interests I had was learning about the food culture."

When she was 15, the family moved to Key West, where she spent her high school years.

"That was pretty neat. We lived on the water and did a lot of fishing, snorkeling, and diving for lobster."

Shortly thereafter, she joined the Air Force.

"I thought it would just be something to do. I remember telling my parents I was simply going to take a test to see what jobs I might qualify for and thought I would be home for dinner. I ended up enlisting and leaving for basic training in Texas that same day.

I didn't feel I was ready to go to college. I didn't really know what I wanted to do. I wanted to travel. I didn't really have the means to do it. So I figured that would be a good way to do it.

I also remember calling home after I got my first duty assignment to Zaragoza Air Base, Spain. I was gone for two years. I didn't think I would end up staying on. I ended up staying in 25 years."

***

Through the Perilous Night

John Gaydos was born in Jourdanton, Texas, in 1970.

"My family moved a lot so I have lived in all the southern states, from Texas to South Carolina. My mother was from Myrtle Beach, so we tended to come back there each year. It is where I graduated from."

Gaydos was an Air Force E-4 when he went to Khobar Towers.

"In November of 1995, my shop was notified that we needed volunteers to deploy to Khobar Towers. I was a back shop avionics technician.

We were the first ever deployed AIS (Avionics Intermediate Shop). My wife was also in my shop and we had a newborn baby girl and a son who has just turned two. Our shop was very small so we thought everyone would have to take a turn being deployed. But the shop was looking for one person to do back-to-back tours so they could be a liaison to the second group to make the transition smoother.

My wife and I talked about it and I volunteered to take both tours so that she would not have to deploy. This would also allow our children to stay with one parent for continuity. Otherwise we would have to get a relative to watch them while she flew to Saudi to relieve me. It just looked like it would work better.

In January of 1996, the families were sending us off at the deployment center. We were all in a small room where we were double checking our baggage and saying farewells. I had a feeling come over me that was so real and vivid that I had to tell my wife. I told her I thought I was going to die on this deployment. It was a feeling like cold in my bones."

Over The Ramparts We Watched

CHAPTER 3
Broad Stripes, Bright Stars: Daily Life at Khobar Towers

Mostly populated by the Air Force, in addition to Army, Navy, Marines and Department of Defense (DoD) civilians, the Khobar Towers were about a 20-minute drive from the nearest runway.

William Schooley, the munitions specialist, remembers–

> "There were also British and French aircraft there, and their personnel were also housed at Khobar Towers. Additionally the TCNs, or third country nationals, were housed there as well.
>
> The Americans had a sectioned-off portion of Khobar Towers with our own security. Khobar Towers itself was in the city of Dhahran, which is why it was so hard to secure.
>
> In fact there was a large mosque with tall minarets right outside our compound. One of the biggest security concerns were the minarets, which would have made a great sniper's nest.
>
> The Saudi government also would not let us trim back the vegetation on the fence surrounding our area because our women, not in burkas, would offend the citizens of Dhahran."

***

Avionics Technician **John Gaydos** had two rotations to Khobar Towers. The first was not very busy.

> "In fact in my entire six-month deployment we only tested two parts."

"During the first rotation there were seven of us deployed. But as we had realized that there was really no mission for us, the second rotation only had three of us. My two new companions were shown around. With nothing to do I volunteered to go to work and they went to the Oasis most days[1]. I would watch the clock and then head from King Abdul Aziz Air Base back to Khobar Towers, just a few blocks away.

Toward the end of that second rotation the lock down was finally lifted. We were able to go downtown in groups of two. I was going to have to rotate home out of sequence to prevent me from getting a short tour. So I was scheduled to leave about a week before the other two from my shop. That's when I got the call.

I had three weeks or so left in country. I received a call telling me that my newborn daughter had her leg broken in a daycare. It was a spiral fracture indicating abuse. Because of her size, she was placed in a cast from her armpits down both legs to keep her still while the bone healed. My wife told me that to make matters worse she had gotten orders to report to leadership school."

Unfortunately, there was confusion and a lack of cooperation over who could allow Gaydos to return home on humanitarian leave.

"My wife was told that I refused to come home and that if she left leadership school she would be ousted from the military. So my mother-in-law

---

[1] A pool and snack bar on the American side of King Abdul Aziz Air Base.

ended up watching my child who was in a full body cast. That was when I knew I would be leaving the military. I felt betrayed."

***

For **Angel Marsh**, the fuels specialist from Louisiana, an average day in Saudi Arabia involved fueling a variety of planes at King Abdul Aziz Air Base. Sometimes she had to cover her arms due to Saudi customs. Off duty, she spent time at the Khobar Towers recreation center or went downtown with a group.

***

Self-described *"ground rat"* **Mike Dunn** arrived in Saudi Arabia on April 11 of 1996. His first memory:

"It's hot! It's crazy hot! You wore long sleeves to keep yourself cooler. Not a friendly place. It was sandy. There was grit and sand in everything, including the food. Not anywhere I would go on a vacation."

At Khobar Towers, the first three floors of Dunn's building were the compound's medical clinics and offices.

On top of the heat and dust, Dunn was hit with bad news.

"About a month and a half in, my wife tells me she's leaving. Not good. And the kid's only like six months old. And then she actually stopped sending me money – I was relying on her, she was running the checkbook. She was sending me money back from the states, and the money kind of stopped. That was a bad situation. I was really in a bad pinch. I started sneaking into the shower after people were in there and using their soap."

Friends helped him out with necessities. He took to running and exercise to help him cope.

"One of the things I did to try to keep my brain straight was I'd run the perimeter of the compound."

And he still had a job to do.

***

Scott Wolff, the jet engine mechanic, arrived in the spring of 1996.

"I worked day shifts for a while and then I worked nights for a while.

It was just kind of like day-to-day flying. A lot of paperwork and stuff like that. Keeping track of the guys, making sure they were doing all right."

***

Selena Zuhoski, who had grown up in Tampa and Key West, was a Staff Sergeant paralegal assigned as Law Office Manager supporting two Judge Advocate General (JAG) officers. She drafted legal and personnel actions and letters, as well as assisting airmen with claims for personal property lost, damaged or stolen. She also dealt with maintenance of the office's one vehicle.

"With us was a Saudi liaison officer who would typically visit and would sometimes show us around."

***

Scott Coleman celebrated his 24th birthday on June 4th in the Khobar Clinic.

"I was on duty that day. Medics' work-rest was 24-on/48-off, but for our 24-on, we had to stay in the clinic and answer anyone who came to the door.

For our 48-off, you weren't expected to be in the clinic during regular duty hours, but a lot of medics did anyways, just to help out or to stay out of trouble.

I was impressed at all the effort our troops had gone to, to make Khobar Towers not such a bad place after all. I didn't know what all the airmen back at 'The Rock' (Little Rock) were complaining about. The U.S. Air Force really knows how to do a deployment right, as far as I was concerned."

The amenities Coleman referred to include the luxury of local transport.

"We had it lucky in the 4404th Med Group. We had a Chevy Suburban, a pick-up truck, and a Montero Sport at our disposal.

The Montero was reserved for the docs, but us med techs could check out the other vehicles and head to the Al Shula Mall or the TCN (third country national) Mall whenever we were off-duty."

"Third country nationals" was the generic name given to people who were typically from south Asia or other middle-eastern countries. The Al Shula Mall had name-brand stores and was frequented by Saudis. The TCN Mall had non-name brand, non-chain stores "specializing in counterfeit merchandise and cheap knockoffs."

Both malls were a short drive from the Khobar Towers.

"I was amazed at how cheap everything was in Saudi. I think at the time, the exchange rate was about 3.50 or 3.75 riyals to the dollar.

I liked the TCN mall. It was cheap, gritty, and I liked that. I even went to the Al Shula mall a time or two. Me, and another medic ... found a Chinese buffet downtown that had 'all you could eat' lobster tails for 14 riyals. How can you beat that? So, off we went."

Scott remembers the doctors also made sure they got "us medics" involved in fun things.

"Our Medical Group Commander, Lieutenant Colonel Doctor Robert N. Bertoldo, got us invited to the McDonnell Douglas compound (a short drive across town) for supper one night. It was great! And to top it off, some random 'Mc-D' employee at the compound restaurant picked up our entire tab for four docs and eight medics.

When the U.S. Consulate held their Fourth of July celebration in the middle of June, they asked us medics from the Khobar clinic to come over and run their first aid station. All of the U.S. citizens and U.S.-friendly (British, Canadian, etc.) people in the area were invited. It was a regular shindig and the Budweiser was a-flyin'. Hey, we were technically on U.S. soil, but a two-beer limit per person."

While he found things to take pleasure in off duty, Scott also took satisfaction in his work.

"I really enjoyed being a medic. Most of our patients that came through our doors were occupational injuries like cuts needing sutures and heat casualties needing IV fluids pushed. And most of the serious stuff came to our door at the clinic after duty-hours, when there were only two medics staffing the clinic and the flight surgeon was on-call.

One night, an EF-111 Raven crew chief grabbed a live pitot tube (pointed appendage on the aircraft that is used to measure airflow) on his plane and came in with serious burns that turned the top layer of skin in his palm to ash. He couldn't open his hand all the way, but me and Staff Sergeant Brian 'Flex' Null, treated him with Silvadine cream, bandaged him up, gave him some pain meds and sent him on his way.

We responded to a lot of in-flight emergencies. We'd hop in the ambulance and take off out of Khobar Towers for the Ops side. And as you remember, it was a long haul from the Khobar clinic to the flight line. I'm no maintainer, but I know the heat took a toll on our aircraft.

I remember lots of 'hot brakes' calls over the net.

One engine out was pretty common for the C-130s. We usually only headed to the flight line when it was at least two engines out for C-130s, or 'hung missiles' for the fighters, or 'smoke in cockpit', or engine fires, or one engine out on the Ravens or F-15s. I think we had to go through two or three ECPs (Entry Control Points) and two FOD[2] checks to get to where the Crash Fire Rescue units were standing by, and by then, the show was usually over.

One thing I'll say for our flight docs at the Khobar clinic: they kept us involved and were constantly training us to improve our skills.

---

[2] Foreign Object Damage. Anyone entering aircraft operating areas must be sure to secure any loose objects that could be sucked into and damage an aircraft engine.

All of us 4FOXs[3] had our NR-EMT (Nationally Registered Emergency Medical Technician) Basic certification and some of the medics had even more advanced EMT certifications. Even so, the docs were always training us to improve our technique on clinical skills usually reserved for nurses. Skills like suturing, starting IVs, phlebotomy (drawing blood), minor surgical techniques, basic life support, and so on. We would practice sewing towels together to get our suture knot-tying techniques down when things got slow.

When patients needed more in-depth diagnostics the medics usually took them to the Saudi Ministry of Defense & Aviation (MODA) hospital on the far side of the airbase.

It was about a 30-minute drive down the Saudi interstate with nothing but sand all the way there. We'd take our patient in the clinic Suburban and really open that thing up. We would floor it most of the way, just because we could and there was hardly anyone else on the road. That same MODA hospital would pay a key role following the attack.

The MODA hospital was staffed mostly by Europeans and Canadian nurses and physicians.

We managed to get invited to a party in a compound, hosted by a Brit civilian.

Myself, Senior Airman Chrisanna Brothers, PJ[4] Staff Sergeant Sean Casey, and a couple other PJs called a cab to the ECP at Khobar and off we went.

---

[3] An Air Force specialty code

[4] Para-rescue man, sometimes called "parachute jumper" and hence, "PJ."

Getting there was an adventure. The cab driver spoke zero English, but we made it to the address the civilian nurse gave to me. We got in the door and the first thing she asked was, 'Did you bring any bacon?'

She must have assumed airmen stationed at Khobar had access to some mythical United States Military Training Mission (USMTM) Commissary Bacon Vault, which was not the case. They still were happy to see us. It was a cozy little illegal party in Dhahran, complete with darts, American country music, home-brewed ale, and boot-leg Jack Daniels. At the end of the night, our hostess hailed us an English-speaking cabby and we staggered back through the ECP, safe and sound.

I was not back on-duty at the clinic until 0700 the next day, so after supper, I went back to my room and started doing laundry around 2000 or so. It was June 25th.

Good thing I had all that practice suturing. You all know what happened next."

***

Larry Oliver, of the security police, arrived at the Khobar Towers housing area in Dhahran, Saudi Arabia on 8 May in 1996. This was a temporary duty (TDY) from Eglin AFB, Florida in support of Operation Southern Watch for a 90-day rotation.

"We arrived late at night, about 11p.m. and went directly to bed'" he recalled. "In the morning, I arose to the sounds of birds chirping and the sweltering heat of a Middle East day.

I was hungry so I made my way to the Desert Rose Dining Hall and actually met some people I had been stationed with at previous locations. It seemed this was going to be yet another one of those trips where you do your job, have some fun and keep an eye on the rotators to reunite with old friends.

Newly assigned personnel worked with CE (Civil Engineering) filling sand bags, building the M-60 machinegun bunkers at the entry road, installing concertina wire around the perimeter, moving jersey barriers and other duty for two weeks as they rotated into country. The main threats they knew of were possible attacks by rocket propelled grenades (RPG's) from the highway that crossed between Khobar and the King Abdul Aziz Air Base.

Additionally, we were warned of threats from a vehicle attempting to run the gate packed with explosives. We did what we could to 'harden' the entry to the base as well as the perimeter. This work took a while, but rotating Security Policemen (SP's) into the AOR did this job for two weeks each to prepare the base in the event of an attack."

Oliver remembers the main gate entrance had two M-60 machinegun bunkers, built atop concrete walls, arranged to give an escape route in case of an RPG attack. The walls facing the highway were approximately three to four feet thick, made of sand bags.

"The M60's were on a one-half load,[5] and should the gate personnel sound the alarm - hand held radio or horn - the M-60's were to fire cyclic

---

[5] An M-60 machinegun on half-load means the ammunition is in the feed tray. To shoot, the gunner has to pull the charging handle back, put the selector on 'FIRE' and press the trigger.

until the vehicle threat had been repelled or stopped entirely. Behind the bunkers were twin 2 ½-ton trucks. If any attacking vehicle survived a dash through two firing M-60 machineguns, drivers would roll the trucks to block the road, keeping any attacking vehicle from getting through to the living areas.

We all knew those trucks were the last line of defense for the main gate and took it very seriously. As a matter of fact, Lieutenant Colonel James Traister (commander of the Security Police Squadron) had routine drills with the trucks and personnel to ensure it would work as advertised. This was also demonstrated to other Wing leaders."

The perimeter was lined inside and out with jersey barriers spaced about a foot away from each other. Between the barriers and the 8-foot fence was a triple strand of concertina wire. Then there was constant patrolling of the inner perimeter by armed Security Police. The outer perimeter was the sole responsibility of the Saudi *"Red Hats"* as the U.S. troops called them.

Oliver recalled that three or four weeks into the deployment:

> "There was a suspicious object found in Building 129's elevator shaft. The building was evacuated and a cordon was established around the building.
>
> I was one who could not get in my own building (129) so I remember this well. I was not working and had just returned from the finance building obtaining cash. Once it was cleared, we returned. I cannot recall the duration of the situation at Building 129 apart from being a few hours.

I cannot remember the exact dates here but this is what was happening. LPOPs (Listening & observation posts) were put atop select buildings within the Khobar Towers complex. These had views of all points on a compass and while posted on these LPOPs, we did view nightly 'activity' outside of the perimeter.

These activities included women – at least individuals dressed in black outfits – pushing on the jersey barriers, sitting on them, vehicles slowly driving by, vehicles attempting to move the barriers on the sandy roads, etc. And as we witnessed these events, we up-channeled these to our supervisors.

There was an order from the Air Force Chief of Staff and the Air Force Security Police Commander to conduct video surveillance of these probes. After each shift, we would turn in whatever tape/notes we had to the Security Police (SP) Law Enforcement Desk (LED). I believe this continued up to the attack and afterward. If we saw something or someone, we would call it in to LED and a patrol would be dispatched, as well as notifying the Saudi's to get them to respond and move whomever or whatever out of the area.

We knew we were being probed and ultimately, something bad happening was inevitable."

The day before the attack, after work, Larry and others decided to go to the Oasis pool during the day to enjoy some time off. The 58th Fighter Squadron from Eglin AFB was due to rotate home on June 26, 1996. The F-15's were flying low overhead returning from their Combat Air Patrol missions in Iraq and were celebrating their departure.

"There was truly a jovial attitude of accomplishment and impending rotation back stateside.

We spent the day lying in the sun, swimming and simply enjoying our precious time off. Later that day, we decided that since we were allowed to go to downtown Dhahran, we would do that for the evening. We signed out of the base at the Law Enforcement Desk and headed to the main gate.

As we hailed a taxi, we talked with one gate SP and he stated that the traffic was unusually light and if we could, to bring him some food from off-base. We agreed, thought nothing of it and departed in the taxi.

The general directive was to move quickly, get what you need, do not loiter and return ASAP. We needed to be in groups of three to five people as to not become an easy target for an abductor for a hostage, nice target for a shooting, etc.

When we got downtown, we cruised through a TCN Mall and ended up at a Saudi shopping mall shortly afterward. We did some haggling but I do not believe any one of us actually purchased anything other than food. We took our time and relaxed, contrary to what we had been told to do. We watched the Saudi people for a while, talked and eventually decided that we would get some McDonald's from the Saudi mall and return to Khobar."

Oliver and his group returned to the main gate approximately 9:35 p.m., gave the SP his dinner "and shot the breeze" for a few minutes.

"An SP was on patrol that night and asked us if we wanted a ride back to our building -129- but we declined. It was a nice night out, not terribly hot or humid, I recall calling it a beautiful night.

We walked back and on the way, the girl I was with wanted to see a friend of hers who was working in the chow hall, so we agreed that we would meet up after I signed us back into the base at the Law Enforcement Desk."

Building 129 sat directly south of Building 131, the structure that would take the brunt of the blast.

Map Showing Relative Location of Khobar Towers, Persian Gulf, Air Base and Dhahran

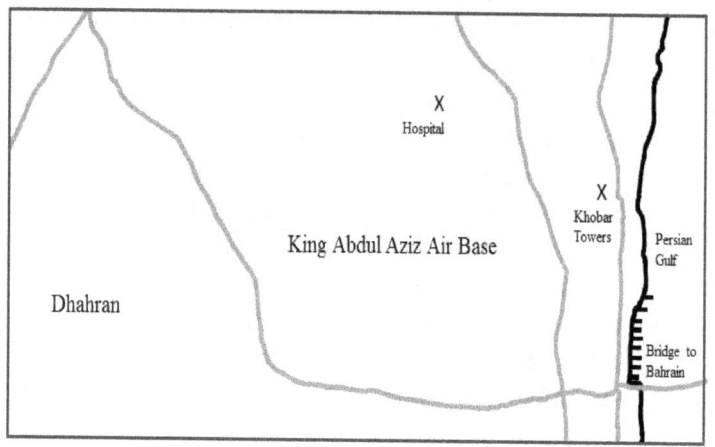

Through the Perilous Night

Map of Khobar Towers Housing Complex

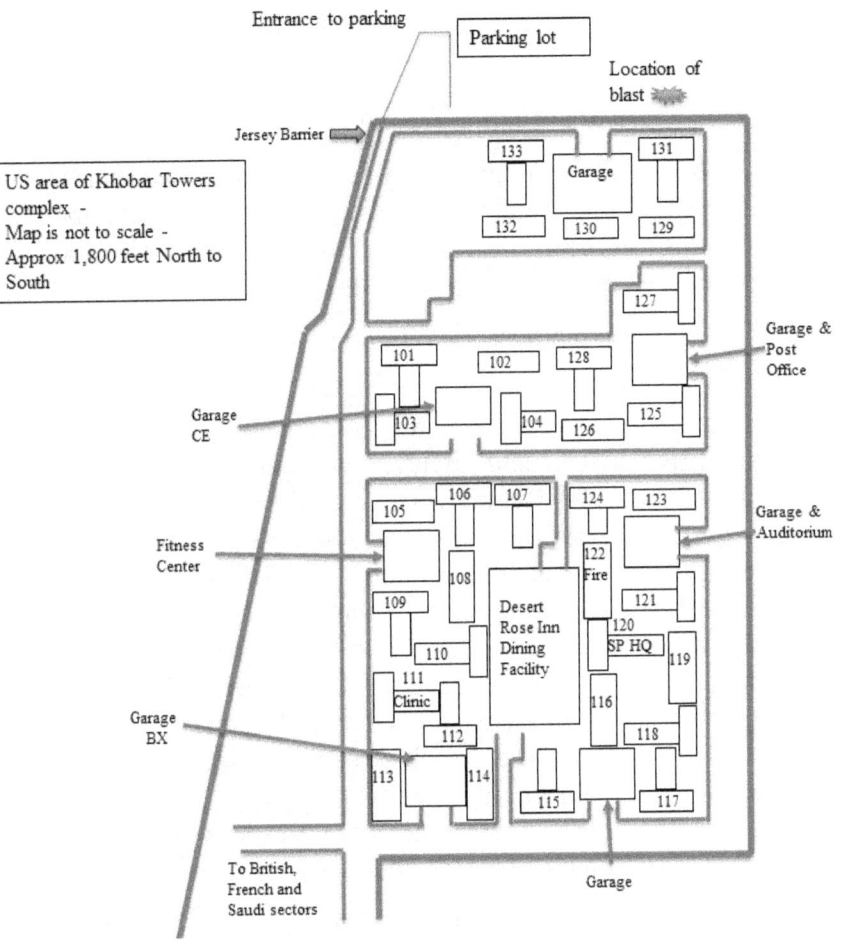

***

Leighton Reid, the disaster preparedness specialist, saw things in terms of his experience and training. He did not like what he saw, he recalled thinking shortly after he arrived.

"I had that sinking feeling, this is not right,"

The towers, a group of more than 70 buildings, belonged to the Saudi government. Thirty-five of the buildings had been turned over to the Air Force and converted to offices and apartments. As far as comfort–

"It was the best TDY (temporary duty) I'd ever been on."

He had a private room with hot and cold showers, a shared living room and kitchen, and his duty office – the Survival Recovery Center (SRC) – on the same floor.

While the comfort factor was good, it was the "sinking feeling" he got at the overall situation that got his attention. Between the buildings and the area outside the base was a strip of grass, a two-lane road, some more grass, concrete four-foot-tall "Jersey Barriers" and an eight-foot chain link fence topped by concertina wire.

That was all there was between the airmen and the outside, a distance of perhaps 80 feet. Immediately outside the fence, nearest his own tower, was a large parking lot for a mosque still under construction.

"That's when all the hair went up on the back of my neck."

He discussed, with his superiors, the possibility of moving the Jersey barriers from other structures within the Khobar compound to set them up in double rows inside of the fence, thereby increasing the protection of the perimeter. He also paid attention to lessons learned from the April 19, 1995, bombing of the federal building in Oklahoma City. The increased security measures and the recovery lessons learned from Oklahoma City likely saved lives. One theme that keeps running through the memory of several survivors: It could have been worse.

The day before the bombing, Reid called home to wish his daughter a happy 20th birthday. In spite of the happy occasion, he felt the shadow of disaster.

"I just had that feeling ... (that I was calling) essentially to say goodbye."

Late that evening he was preparing for a change of command scheduled for 9 a.m. the next day, also for a meeting with his Saudi counterparts to coordinate a joint exercise.

***

Jessica Bradshaw, the SP who had originally been at the bottom of the deployment list, was a senior airman (E4) when she arrived in Dhahran – an "interesting" rank because she was neither an airman first class nor a staff sergeant.

"As a senior airman, you are provided more challenges to ensure you are prepared to join the NCO ranks."

As with others, one big impression was the heat.

"I would use the Zest soap, and as soon as you would walk outside you're already gross and sweating."

She and her fellow airmen were "always doing something on our day off." At the air base at Dhahran, there was an Olympic sized pool. There were also trips downtown. At Khobar–

"I used to rollerblade the perimeter all the time."

Bradshaw and other security forces lived in Building 129, separated from Building 131, by an outdoor covered patio area. Her building had just three or four stories instead of eight like Building 131, did. Her room was on the second floor.

"The dorms were awesome. When you first enter my living quarters you open a door and there was a bedroom located on the left side. As you continue down the hallway, there was a kitchen and laundry room located on the right side. There was a door at the end of this hallway that opened into the lounge area. The lounge area contained a television, furniture, end tables, and a balcony with a sliding glass door.

To get to my bedroom you would continue through the lounge area and make a right at the end of the hallway. My bedroom was the first room on the right side, all the way in the back."

The security police squadron had a separate building for the armory and duty desk. That building was near the Desert Rose dining facility.

***

Lieutenant Colonel **Doug Cochran**, the commander of the 58th Fighter Squadron, was not new to Saudi Arabia.

"I had been deployed to Saudi in 1994 as the Operations Officer of the 59th Fighter Squadron, but I felt the Saudis were much more difficult to work with on this deployment.

We continued to have jet maintenance problems but our folks did amazing work getting our jets in the air and we never missed a combat sortie.

There had been a bombing in the capital of Riyadh six months prior. It was a 250-pound car bomb which killed several people. The Saudi officials rounded up several suspects and promptly proceeded to behead them - before any of our officials like the FBI could interview them for more intel[6].

The Khobar housing complex where we lived was sealed down and additional security was implemented.

During the deployment at wing standups, intel reports were stating that there was possibly a growing threat to allied forces. We were ready for a similar attack such as the one in Riyadh during the previous November. Everyone was being very vigilant and reported several suspicious activities.

The night of the attack we were two days from most of our personnel redeploying back home. I had just finished cleaning my room and bathroom in preparation for our replacement squadron from Langley."

***

Tennessean **Trena Schmidt** had been working day shifts with occasional 12-hour shifts. Her barracks were near the chow hall, the Desert Rose.

On the afternoon of June 25, Schmidt had gone to the gym for a workout, then to the Khobar recreation area

---

[6] Intel = intelligence

where people could play games, cards, listen to music or just relax.

"Around about 9 or 9:30 p.m., I came back to my barracks," the 7th floor of her tower, Schmidt remembered. "I showered and then talked to some of the other girls in my suite. I went to bed a little bit before 10."

***

Although the location of **Leighton Reid's** room and office in Building 133 was called the "ground floor," this was still about five feet above the ground, which afforded him a small balcony. He stepped out on the balcony for a smoke and saw Air Force Captain Sandra Beneway out for a jog. Looking up as she passed, she called out:

"Sergeant Reid, don't you ever get out of that uniform?"

Reflecting on that, Reid went to his room and changed into shorts, flip-flops and a white T-shirt printed with a reproduction of the "*Far Side*" newspaper comic with a map showing a location as "the middle of nowhere."

Back in his office, he looked out the window about 9 p.m. and saw a white pickup truck, outside the Jersey Barriers, pulled up onto grass at the edge of the parking lot outside the compound. The driver stood outside the vehicle. The vehicle faced to Reid's left, toward the parking lot. It was about 250 to 300 feet away, opposite Building 131, to Leighton's east.

"He was smoking, probably worse than I was. I was trying to keep my eyes on him and he's got his beads on me."

Reid stepped back out to the balcony to light another cigarette, found that he'd left his lighter inside. As he turned to go back, the driver got back into the pickup and flashed his lights three times.

***

At around the same time, about 200 yards south of Reid (and 300 yards from the pickup truck), **William Schooley** had also stepped out for a smoke.

"The memories of what happened on June 25, 1996 are still very vivid to me and I'm sure I will never forget what happened that night.

I was standing on the balcony smoking a cigarette. My suite mates and I had just finished watching '*Broken Arrow*.' Not much of a movie really, Hollywood can't seem to ever get the military right. The others had left to go about their nightly rituals of showers or just personal time.

I glanced down at my watch and noted that it was ten o'clock, I put out my cigarette thinking that I was an hour late for bed, having just come off my shift. I was trying desperately to get my sleep schedule straightened out. No matter what hours you are used to, the Air Force always has a different schedule in mind. I came in the sliding glass doors and struggled to get them closed. The rollers had long since given up their useful lives."

Meanwhile, in his own office, **Reid** saw that his laptop, which he thought had shut down earlier, was still going through the shutdown process. He sat at the military issue gray steel desk watching the laptop to ensure that it shut all the way down. He heard the distinctive sound of a large Mercedes diesel vehicle drive by outside. He thought it was the engineers responding to a water main breakage that had occurred earlier that day.

***

Michael Willis, the communications specialist, remembered that after the bus ride that had taken him from work to his building - past the old fuel truck that struck him as a potential place to conceal an explosive –

"I went to my room that was on the other side of the compound from Building 131. There was a person watching TV in the day room and I sat down to join him.

I was sitting on a couch that just happened to be directly facing the rear of Building 131, through a sliding glass door. The other person was sitting in at a 90-degree angle from me and directly facing the TV. We talked and complained about the lack of movie choices on the TV.

After about an hour I decided to go to bed. My room was actually directly behind where I had been sitting. I was lying in bed and reading my Bible when it happened."

***

Earlier that evening, **Mike Dunn** was getting ready to go on a run:

"The night that the bomb went off, I had actually walked down there and I was standing – this is significant because of the way it's laid out. The thinnest part of the compound, where it's most exposed, that's part of the track, one leg of it.

So I go out, I stretch, I get ready to run, and then I'm just like, not tonight."

Dunn went to the gym instead, where he worked out with a "cheap, fast workout" of 15-20 minutes.

"Had I been out running then, I might not be here talking to you today. I'm glad I didn't take that run."

Dunn headed back to his building, which was "about four blocks" from the location of the explosive-carrying truck.

"One of my workmates, one of the females from the squadron that I work in, catches me in the lobby by her suite. She wanted to ask me some questions about the phone in her room. She kind of equates that I'm in communications so maybe I work on the phone system."

Dunn had to pause while telling his story.

"When I lead up to it, it's kind of hard to breathe."

A moment later, he said–

"We're having this conversation and the light above my head flickers."

***

At his post on top of Building 131, directly facing the bomb vehicle, Staff Sergeant Alfredo R. Guerrero correctly interpreted the suspicious activity of the men and white pickup below as a threat. He raced into the building to launch evacuation.

As Mike Dunn and the airman were talking about the phone in her room, about 15 feet and on the other side of the wall from where Leighton Reid sat, there was a speaker in the control center monitoring radio calls. Reid heard cryptic shouts over the speaker, followed a minute later by what he thought were three rifle cracks.

Then it began.

CHAPTER 4
The Perilous Night

On the evening of June 25, **Jessica Bradshaw** remembers-

"After work I took a shower, tossed on sandals, shorts and a T-shirt and we went to play volleyball."

She got back to her dorm about 9:40 p.m.

"I never watch TV. This is the weirdest thing. So I came back to the dorm room and the worst smell ever was there in the dorm room, like rotten eggs."

She tried to close the sliding glass door to cut off the odor, but it would not shut all the way. "OK, I'm stuck with this all night," she thought.

"I go into my room to go to bed and I look at the clock. It's about 9:54. And I turn around in my door frame and think, no, I'm going to go watch TV. Then I thought, no, I never watch TV."

She changed her mind again and started out of her room.

"I had my hand in the doorframe when the bomb went off. I thought it was a sandstorm. Because it lasted seconds. You could hear the noise. You could see glass circulating in the air, which I thought was sand at the time. It was like thunder or a very loud airplane engine sound. It lasted seconds. And then it was just pitch black."

***

When the light above **Mike Dunn** and the airman flickered—

"We both stop talking and look up at it, and it flickers again, real hard. And then it just comes back on steady.

I took a look at the light and then I looked down at her and I go to say something like, that was weird or spooky or something like that, and the blast wave hit.

It blew out glass everywhere. And the ground was shaking. I kind of pushed her into another room and kind of jumped in there with her."

***

Paralegal **Selena Zuhoski** was watching a movie when the bomb detonated.

"I was relaxing with friends in the Recreation Center after playing volleyball. A comedy was playing on the television and there were about 30 people sitting on chairs and sofas around the TV. I was sitting at a round table.

Suddenly, the lights in the room flickered and I saw what looked like smoke blow in through the tiny windows along the top of one wall. Then the lights went out briefly.

The blast had picked me up and thrown me into a wall. Apparently I had lost consciousness and the next thing I know a co-worker was talking to me and helping me to my feet."

***

John Gaydos, still hoping to return to his wife and injured child, was in the common day room on the fifth floor of Building 130.

Through the Perilous Night

> "I was laying on a couch watching a TV show about a guy who lived with bears in Alaska. I was waiting to see him get eaten (he did a few years later).
>
> At 9:50 p.m., I felt a concussion. I would later realize it was the primary detonation of the truck bomb.
>
> I sat up off the couch in time to see the main detonation. The entire parking lot of the Mosque next door seemed to rise into the air. It was sparkling and twinkling."

Then the blast wave hit.

> "Our day room had sliding glass doors. They were closed and two of my roommates were outside on the balcony talking about guns. Those windows blew in and I put my left arm up to shield myself from the flying glass and debris. It seemed like the wind and roar of the detonation lasted forever but it could only have been a second or two."

***

At the same time, for fuels specialist **Angel Marsh**, life went abruptly from a day she did not recall much of to one of deadly violence.

> "I don't remember a whole lot of what I did … I think I was working … I do know that day they had just told us that starting this weekend you all can start doing the Bahrain trips. They had stopped them for a while. And so everybody was excited about that.
>
> That night, I was actually out on my balcony. It was like a big apartment building, everybody had a balcony.

I was out smoking, I was going back in, I was about to take a shower and get ready for bed. I had closed the door, a sliding glass door. My hand was still on the curtain when the bomb went off."

***

Heading to the Law Enforcement Desk, **Larry Oliver** walked in through the glass doors directly in front of the elevator doors, turned right and attempted to sign himself and the others back in. He was about 450 yards south of the vehicle that was stuffed with explosives.

"Shortly after my entry, an airman I supervised, I no longer remember the name, had entered to check his mail, turned left to go to the mailboxes. As I attempted to sign us in, of course there was no pen. At approximately 2152 hours, I turned to ask the LED desk sergeant for a pen and that is when it hit."

***

At that same instant—

"I knew immediately what was going down," **Leighton Reid** said.

Recalling his Army brother-in-law's advice that "if something is happening, get your ass down," he attempted to hit the floor but didn't quite make it. A blast, heat and shockwave hit him from the front and then from behind and "threw me into the desk head first." He saw stars.

"I moved that hundred-pound desk about a foot and a half with my head."

***

Simultaneously, **Squadron Commander Doug Cochran**—

"was standing at my desk, my left side about one to two feet from the window to my room. My room was on the top, 8th floor of Building 127, two buildings directly behind Building 131, about 400 feet from the blast.

At just before 10 p.m., local time, the ground shook and my window totally exploded, throwing me across the room and I landed face down on the opposite side of the room.

I froze in that position thinking the building was going to collapse and the best way to survive would be to lie flat. After a moment, I realized the building would stand a bit longer and I immediately did a finger and toes check and then called out to my suite mates to see if they were all right. I remember not being able to hear myself as I called out - later realizing I was temporarily deaf and a combination of having the air sucked out of my lungs because of the super pressurization of the blast.

I crawled out to the living room to find my two roommates, both alive, but one had a huge glass dagger sticking out of his thigh."

Cochran and the uninjured roommate quickly tended to him and then helped him evacuate the building.

"I was still convinced that the building was going to collapse at any moment."

***

Meanwhile, **William Schooley** had just walked through the living room and into his bedroom / dining room and began to clean up the trash left over from packing. He was scheduled to leave on Thursday.

"This had been a long and miserable TDY and I was very happy to be going home.

Without warning the whole room began violently shaking. I will remember this horrible rumbling sound for the rest of my life, unbelievably loud in intensity. Having lived in California, I thought it was an earthquake at first.

An empty gray metal wall locker, which served to section off the room between my room-mate and I, began to shimmy its way across the room towards me. Not knowing where to seek sanctuary I laid down on my bed and curled up in a ball, with my arms and hands instinctively encircling my head for protection. Time slowed and the rumbling and shaking continued on and on. I began to think this can't possibly be an earthquake; it must be a SCUD (missile).

My mind was racing, the rumbling and shaking continued. I began to feel afraid, I kept thinking … *'Make it stop! Oh God please make it stop.'* The wall locker fell on top of me; I shoved it off, *'Please, please make it stop!'*

All at once the chaos subsided, what had seemed like minutes had only been a few seconds. I first made sure I wasn't injured, and then climbed over the other four wall lockers which had tumbled over, through the door and out into the hallway. My first thought being to check on my suite mates."

***

At the moment of the explosion, **Trena Schmidt**—

"wasn't asleep when the bomb went off. I was just lying in bed, and then all of a sudden the room started to rumble.

For a real split second, I thought it was an earthquake. But then just shortly after that, I knew it wasn't an earthquake. I thought we were being bombed by airplanes.

The room was shaking and rumbling. The building was moving. The window lit up like it was daylight. It was very loud. It seemed like, when the room lit up, the walls came in and went back out. It seemed like this lasted a long time."

***

Scott Wolff remembers a moment between realizing something was wrong and the blast. Wolff was on the fourth floor of Building 130, facing and overlooking a parking garage. To the east of the parking garage, northeast of Wolff's building, was Building 131, the building directly opposite the blast.

"I was getting ready to go to work when the light went out. A few seconds later the blast hit.

The window blew in, showering me with glass fragments and the metal frame. I could hear a rumbling noise, not sure what the sound was, my first thought was my building was falling down on top of me. I ducked and covered."

***

But for **Michael Willis**, it wasn't immediately apparent what had happened.

"At first I thought someone slammed my door for some reason. When I got up I saw the door was blown off the hinges and there was glass everywhere. I remember it being completely silent for what seemed like an hour but was probably no more than five seconds. Then the yelling and screaming started."

***

At the Law Enforcement desk, searching for that elusive pen, **Larry Oliver** remembers the lights "browning out," the building starting to shake and someone shouting to get on the floor.

"I looked up and could see the concrete dust coming out of the cracks of the concrete ceiling. The constant banging sounded like the elevator was falling and hitting every floor on the way down. I recall yelling an expletive and stayed in place on the floor until the shaking stopped.

Afterward, I got up, dusted myself off and moved over to look at the elevators. What I saw, I could not understand. I thoroughly expected to see the elevator doors split and damaged.

What I saw was glass impaled into the metal elevator doors and concrete walls. I did not understand until I turned toward the doors and saw the contorted frames blown in with glass everywhere. Directly in line of sight was a huge 'mushroom' cloud beyond what I suspected was my building, 129.

That is when it all began to make sense."

***

When Willis had thought he heard a door slam, **Dusty Huntley**, the fuel specialist—

"was in the bathroom just finishing shaving and putting all my toiletries away when I heard a loud BOOM. I started turning towards the window to see what happened when I heard a second.

That was when a concussion blew through the window, shattering it and throwing me against the door. Luckily, I turned just in time otherwise I would have had a face full of glass.

The lights went out and the air was full of dust and debris. I opened the door to the sound of screams and loud voices. I called out to see if everyone was okay. That's when I heard someone say '*Get downstairs now.*'

As we made our way down the stairs we were checking each floor as we went. I met up with one of our female airmen, Patricia Goldman, who was injured and to what extent I wasn't sure. But I carried her down the remaining three flights of stairs and to where a temp triage was beginning to form at the direction of our Flight Chief and First Sergeant. I started to perform self-aid and buddy care on her and one other of our wounded airman, Paul Ooten."

***

The force of the blast struck **Angel Marsh** before she had a chance to close the balcony curtain.

"I flew from right in front of that door, over the couch, into the opposite wall. I remember there was a girl in my suite sitting right next to the sliding glass door, but not in front of it, kind of in the corner. And I made eye contact with her and it was kind of like slow motion. I'm just looking at her, freaking out.

I got up after I landed. I stood up, and by that time other people were coming out of their rooms. And I was like, 'what was that?' And they're like, 'I don't know, but get out of here!'

At that point, I got up and I don't know what made me stop. I stopped in my room and grabbed my sandals because I didn't have any shoes on, because I was about to go and take a shower.

So I had those in my hand and I started going down the stairs. But I was hurting – at this point I didn't know what was hurt, or cut, or anything, but I was kind of limping down the stairs."

Another airman from two floors above, making his way down the stairs, saw that she was hurt.

"He actually ended up picking me up and carrying me the rest of the way out of the building. I kept yelling at him, because I was like, *'You can't carry me, I weigh too much!'*

We got out of the building. Nobody really knew what to do. Everybody kind of gathered by the chow hall, just kind of standing around. Everybody was just kind of still in shock."

***

Paralegal **Selena Zuhoski** got to her feet with the help of a co-worker.

"I found out later that my head had hit the wall hard enough to cause what the doctors called Traumatic Brain Injury (TBI).

This injury would eventually lead to seizures and a diagnosis of temporal lobe epilepsy.

I made my way outside and it was dark, but I could see a large, mushroom-shaped cloud of smoke behind and near the building where my office was located. I grabbed a flashlight out of the the glove box of the JAG's vehicle.

Then we heard someone calling from a window in the next building. He said 'Hey, there's a guy up here on the 4th floor dying.'

I ran there and there was a picnic table and other debris blocking the door. We cleared the debris and carried the man down on a door that had been blown off its hinges. We placed him on the table where I stayed and provided first aid but it did not help.

He died while I attempted to stop bleeding that was coming from a gaping chest wound he had suffered in the explosion."

***

John Gaydos, still in the fifth-floor day room of Building 130, thought the base had been hit by a SCUD missile.

"I headed for my room to get my web gear with my gas mask and supplies. Looking back, I laugh because I had no filter for my gas mask, they weren't issued. In my rush, I slipped on some glass and slammed headfirst into a concrete wall. I fell to my knees and quickly recovered. I tried opening the door to my room but couldn't. I began kicking but it wouldn't budge.

That is when my shop chief came into the day room from his room. He was asking if everyone was OK. We all said yes. But H.G. And T.T. (names withheld) were still on the balcony. Later, in shock, I would think they had died. It would be days before I accepted that they had survived.

There were no lights left in our building. I took my shop chief and made him turn so I could check him by moonlight. He looked fine, nothing life threatening. He then asked me to do the same. I had barely started turning before he told me we had to get me to the clinic.

In his bare feet he walked and helped me get over the blown-out doors of our apartment and begin to go down the stairwell. He was helping me walk, I didn't know why I couldn't do it on my own. I began to do a digit check. I wiggled each finger and toe as we walked. I could feel them all. I reached with my right hand and felt my left ear. Then I reached for my right ear and all I felt was wetness and my hand slide into it.

I began screaming. I thought part of my head was gone. He turned me in the moonlight that was streaming through a tiny hole where a window had been. He grabbed my hand and pulled it back. I had missed my ear and stuck my fingers into a cut where my skin had been peeled back when I slipped headfirst into the wall. He placed my hand over the cut and I could feel my ear with the tips of my fingers.

We made it down a floor or two before we saw a group of people trying to give an unconscious person CPR. There was another guy in a corner by the elevator. He was clearly in shock because he was holding a notebook or clipboard saying over and over 'this wasn't in the schedule.' My shop chief told me to keep going for the clinic. He then began CPR on the unconscious person. I only made it a few steps before I realized I could not go on alone.

I went back up the steps and asked for help. My shop chief had snapped the others out of the shock and they took up where he left off. He then began helping me on my journey again."

***

When the "shaking and rumbling" finished, **Trena Schmidt**—

"jumped up and ran to the door of my room that went into the common area...

There was a girl that had been in the shower, a community shower. There was a window in the shower, a real small window. It blew that window in, and it blew her out of the bathroom. Blew that door open. She was laying on the floor bleeding.

Some of the other girls ran out of their rooms at the same time.

It was dark. Some grabbed flashlights. Broken glass was laying all around, sheetrock was hanging from the ceiling.

People were yelling and screaming. We tried to get her up. She was able to get up on her own."

Others grabbed a robe and shoes for the injured airman from the shower. Schmidt went back to her own room to get a pair of flip-flops.

"My feet were cut up some, and my legs."

After accounting for everyone–

"some were saying we needed to grab our chem[7] warfare masks. But we didn't. I didn't grab mine. I didn't think I needed to."

---

[7] Chem = chemical

Schmidt and the others went into the hall. Bypassing the 7th-floor elevators, they met others leaving their suites and starting down the stairs.

"They were screaming and crying. People were hardly dressed. Some had their chem masks and helmets on. Some were injured. Some weren't.
Outside, people were running and screaming."

Survivors moved toward the Desert Rose parking lot where they began to set up a triage area.

"Other people were running in the opposite direction, toward Building 131. At the time, we didn't know it was a truck bomb."

***

Mike Dunn, whose first inkling of something wrong had been flickering lights, and the airman he saved were joined by two other women in the suite who came into the common area, stunned.

"We're kind of freaking out. It's dark. I thought maybe a plane had gone down."

Remembering that the emergency protocol was evacuate to the Desert Rose, the three headed that way.

"We start going down the stairwell. It's dark, you can hear crackling under your feet. You're just walking on glass and trying to feel your way down through this tunnel, the stairwell.
While we're walking away from the medical building, naturally everyone who's been hurt and is still able to move themselves is making their way to the medical building.
All of a sudden I start seeing these people, and they're walking by, and they're injured or wounded.

There's people dragging other people ... it's like you're watching TV, like you're watching something else happen that you're not really part of. You're just a viewer of all this."

Dunn and his group continued to the Desert Rose, where they were locked down.

"We're all just trying to process and stay calm. "

***

Meanwhile, **Leighton Reid** was not sure how long he lay on the floor, where his head had hit and moved his desk, before he noticed shattered glass everywhere. The blast had blown all the doors off their hinges including the door jambs. He made his way to a hallway blocked by a heavy display case. Despite being all of 5 feet 6 inches tall and weighing about 135 pounds, he picked it up and shoved it out of his way.

"I don't know how I managed to do that."

***

Immediately after realizing what had happened, Security Policeman **Larry Oliver** and two others went through the contorted frames over the glass and down the stairs to the armory window. There he pounded on it until the armorer opened the window.

"He opened the window and asked what the hell had just happened. We demanded our M-16 rifles after shortly explaining with expletives what had just occurred. We received our M-16's, put the magazines in and released the bolt thus chambering a round. We had been hit, game on.

Shortly, seconds to a minute afterward, the Chief and Operations Officer gathered us there to get body armor, Kevlar helmets, etc. from the mobility NCO so we could respond.

Here we were, dressed in civilian clothes, carrying M-16 rifles in partial body armor - by choice - responding to the scene of the attack. Speed was essential."

***

Scott Wolff recalled—

"When the noise stopped, I could hear my suite mates calling out to make sure I was all right. I pulled my pants up and started heading to the stairwell but in the darkness I had to push stuff out of my path.

I went back in to my room and got my flashlight. Heading back toward the stairwell, I could see furniture blown back towards the center wall. I pushed it aside and got to the hall. My suitemates were going down the steps, which were very slippery. Looking down, I could see they were covered in blood.

I assisted one of them out of the building because he was weak from blood loss from a big cut on the right side of his face and neck. When we got outside, there were a lot of my fellow squadron members, including some of my supervisors.

One of the airmen said to me he had blown up the building. I asked why he thought that. He said he was in the elevator and as soon as he pushed the button he was hit by the blast. The next day we could see the dent, in the shape of his body, in the back of the elevator where he was thrown."

***

Through the Perilous Night

During this same time, **Michael Willis–**

"put on my pants and boots and ran out of my room. The first thing I saw was the person I left still sitting with his legs propped up. His legs were cut pretty bad and he was just sitting there and not moving, but wide awake. I ran to him and shook him. I asked him if he was OK and if he could hear me. He snapped out of his fog and I told him to stay put while I checked on the others in our squadron.

Suddenly two airmen came running into our suite. They were in need of help. Another airman was shaving when the bomb went off and the glass from the mirror had cut him up pretty bad. I told them to apply direct pressure to the arm wounds and get him to the hospital. The hallway was filling up with scared and confused airmen. Thankfully everyone else was in pretty good shape, just some minor cuts."

***

While Willis worked with his group, **Jessica Bradshaw** still in pitch blackness, tried to make sense of what had happened.

"I thought, that was a weird sandstorm, like you see in the movies. That must be what happened.

I go to leave my doorframe and I run into something. Its pitch black. I can't see anything and I'm starting to panic, like, wait a second– there shouldn't be furniture here. I'm walking through the hallway, and there shouldn't be anything here.

So I go to the right and I run into another piece of furniture.

I'm trying to call for help but it felt like I didn't have a voice...

The worst feeling was opening the door to the hallway that would get me to the outside, because in the living room area there was that one door that shut, that I had to walk through the long hallway to get to our outside door to get to the hallway with everyone else. That was really scary for me, because I didn't understand what was going on. It was pitch black, and I was afraid of what was going to be behind this door. Could I even get out? Because I kept running into all this furniture.

So I open the door and I'm still screaming for help but it felt like I was barely screaming. Like I didn't have a voice. So I'm walking through the hallway, I can't see anything, and now there was nothing blocking my way. I was super excited about that."

When she finally opened the door to the stairs, an Airman Curley was there. He asked if there was anyone else in there and she answered—

"No it's just me.
He said – but you were screaming so loud.
It was crazy because it didn't seem like I was screaming that loud at all."

The two of them made their way down the stairs and out – "the elevators had been caved in" – with the help of emergency lights that had come on.

They found an airman who had been in front of the glass doors when the bomb went off. One leg—

"was just all blood. The skin was gone from the knee down."

After helping him out of the building, Curley went back into the building to help others get out. Visibility was somewhat obscured.

"It felt like the dust was settling, like the dust had been disturbed. It was a little hazy and dusty."

Bradshaw borrowed a T-shirt and a sock to tie up the airman's leg wound.

"He definitely did not like that. But that's the only thing we could do."

Then four airmen carried out another victim and laid him on the ground next to her.

"I just remember talking to him, saying hey it's going to be fine, but I didn't look at his wounds, because I knew they were really bad. I just had to focus and not get emotional or upset."

Vehicles drove up and people started loading the wounded. One man drove with a broken arm.

"Then someone starts screaming we're getting attacked – like the locals were jumping the fence. Of course I'm security forces - we had taken care of all the wounded, so let's run and get weapons…

I remember stopping and thinking, *this can't be happening. This is crazy.*"

When she got to the security building, the desk sergeant asked her to help him staff the desk in all the confusion. Seeing that there were two flight chiefs on the desk with him. She declined, telling him–

"I need to be out there with a gun."

Leaving the building, she spotted herself in a mirror.

"I stopped and just looked at myself for a second. Because I'm here with an M16, I chambered the round, I have it on fire, I'm in shorts and a T-shirt and it was just like, it was a little bit surreal, that this was happening.
It was totally crazy."

Having secured their own building, security forces moved out to the perimeter.

Bradshaw borrowed a uniform from an airman first class, junior to her.

"So I kind of demoted myself."

Rumors abounded, including one that locals were pillaging. She got into a disagreement with a staff sergeant who was trying to post one of the airmen from her dorm. The airman was upset about the bodies on one side of Building 129 and she didn't want to be posted there.

"Fear was gone at this point, I was just angry."

***

Meanwhile, after the fellow airman carried her out of her building, **Angel Marsh** said, some kind of commotion suddenly got everyone running.

"I had no idea – I didn't know if we were getting attacked again. At this point I still didn't know what happened. I didn't know if it came from the sky or what. "

After some more chaos and confusion, the group stopped running.

"That's when I noticed I had cuts and stuff."

She told others who wanted to help her that she was OK and she started helping others, who were more seriously injured. A first sergeant called everyone to gather around.

"She started telling us we were going to go back, start cleaning, and just different stuff. And during that, her telling us that, I guess I don't know if I was dehydrated or lost blood or what, I passed out. The last thing I remember, I was trying to tap the guy in front of me, on his shoulder, and I don't know if I ever tapped him or not."

***

As Marsh's group gathered, Squadron Commander **Doug Cochran** evacuated Building 127 with almost all the others.

"We were able to evacuate all but one person. Due to his injuries we could not move him until medical folks tended to him first. We gathered in the adjoining parking lot and performed first aid and buddy care to the injured.

I felt strongly that a bomb had detonated nearby but I had no idea where at this point.

Then someone came running towards us from the direction of Building 131, shouting, 'They are coming through the fence, they are coming through the fence!'

At this point we thought we were under attack from unknown ground forces. So we quickly gathered everyone up and made a quick dash to the interior of the compound.

The attack never materialized, and we later found out it was local Saudi citizens coming to the aid of the injured."

***

Still assisted by his shop chief, **John Gaydos**—

"made it across the gravel parking lot before I realized I was not going to make it. My vision was dimming and even my hearing was starting to go. I made him stop and told him to tell my wife I love her. He asked what and I repeated it before my legs began to buckle.

By this point my vision was a blur and my hearing was barely hearing him scream 'Medic!' I could hear someone saying 'this way' as he carried me toward a bus. I laid down in the aisle and three people took over.

My shop chief began helping with someone else. After helping at accident scenes, I know how hard it is to work on a friend or family versus a stranger.

I remember three people began working on me. One on my left arm, one on my left leg and another talking to me trying to keep me conscious.

I guess by this point my adrenaline was ebbing as I calmed down. But that set me up for going into shock. I got so cold they had to cover me with a blanket. I passed out several times as a severed nerve was touched in my left arm as the medic there tried to adjust his hold to stop the bleeding. I remember waking to CPR compressions on my chest. I was asked where I was from.

When I told the girl who was asking, she said she was from the same town. She knew people I knew. That pulled me back to reality and from slipping into full on shock. It also calmed me to know someone else was there that knew who I knew."

***

Concurrently, **Larry Oliver** and his security group headed for the chow hall.

"Somewhere in this chaos, a group of us met at the Desert Rose after arming for a quick head-count but it was all but impossible. Everyone from every squadron was mixed together.

I remember a crowd of people running at us from the area of the attack believing there was a secondary device. You either ran or got run over. I remember Lieutenant Colonel Traister seemingly looking stunned that we had rifles, loaded, in civilian attire. I honestly do not know if he realized the scope of the attack at that point.

Finally a short period of time afterward, we were ordered to move up to the scene of the attack."

***

While Oliver and his group responded, outside his own building, **Scott Wolff–**

"went over and asked one of the officers if I could go back inside and search for injured, but she did not respond. She was just standing there in shock. So me and another guy went back inside and started searching each suite. About halfway through the search one of the airmen came out and said another airman, nicknamed Stealth, was hurt bad.

I went in the suite and found him squatted down next to a couch with his head between his knees on the floor. Between his feet were his eyeglasses in a puddle of blood.

Me, and the airman, tried to get him up but he was too weak. I went to the stairwell and was met by four soldiers who came in and carried him out in a blanket.

I continued the search but found no other victims. I went back outside, then realized I should have gotten the keys to the bus so we could use it as an ambulance to transport victims to the clinic. I asked the same officer if I could go back inside to retrieve the keys; again, no response so I went back in and got the keys.

We started loading victims on the bus. I had to brush the glass off the seat from the broken windshield and drove the first load to the clinic. I returned to the dorm and picked up another load and drove them to the clinic. I did this about three times.

While unloading at the clinic on one trip, I looked over at the clinic and inside I could see someone on top of a table straddling one of the victims and performing CPR on him. I yelled out the window for someone to shut the curtains because I felt that we didn't need to see that and someone immediately did.

I returned back to the dorm area to see if I could be of further assistance. I went around to the street side of the dorms where I could see the front of the dorm, now knowing what had caused the rumbling noise I had heard earlier. The whole front side of the building next to ours had collapsed."

***

After the initial shock, **Dusty Huntley** saw fear spread through the survivors.

"It wasn't long, before the second wave of panic happened, when a group of Saudi civilians had come through the opening in the fence. We weren't sure what was happening. We just knew panic erupted and I had to help both of my wounded (airmen).

When I turned back to pick up Patricia (Goldman), she had already been swept up, so I helped Paul (Ooten) to wherever it was we ended up.

We finally ended up over in the lawn outside the medical dorm. Patricia wouldn't let me leave her sight from then on, but I had to help carry as many of the hundreds of wounded as possible. There were a few whose wounds looked so severe that I can't get the images out of my mind to this day.

I stayed with Patricia and Paul until they were treated, treating as many I could until that time."

***

Still recovering from the shock, **William Schooley** noticed shards of glass were everywhere; the sliding glass doors were in the middle of the living room.

"I was lucky, two minutes later I would have been standing on the balcony and would have been cut to ribbons by all the glass."

A couple of others came out their rooms.

"Everyone was asking 'are you OK, are you sure?' Once satisfied that no one was injured we began checking the other rooms, to see if anyone else was in the suite. Nothing, everyone else was out.

We then proceeded out to the entry hallway. The bulletin board said, 'In the event of attack, stay in the entryway.' We discussed this briefly and decided that the safest place would be outside. Being on the first floor of an eight-story building seemed like a bad idea.

What if the building came down?

We then noticed the sound of the shower in the small bathroom off the entry. Steve (one of the roommates) banged on the door. My roommate Jeff was in there, he said he was fine and was going to finish his shower. We tried to explain to him the seriousness of the situation and he insisted that he would be out soon."

***

At about the same time, **Leighton Reid** scrambled through darkness and wreckage to his room to retrieve trousers and boots – no socks, just boots to protect his feet. The only light was from trees outside, set on fire by the explosion.

Reid took an emergency light out of his control center into the landing to illuminate the stairwell. Airmen were awkwardly negotiating their way down from the six floors above. Reid used his light to help people find their way out.

"You could see the pools of blood dripping on to the slick marble floors coming down the stairwell," he said. "People were slipping on the blood."

Captain Beneway, the woman who had teased him about being in uniform all the time, was being led down with a pillow held to the side of her head. He found out later that "she had lost half her face." As they steadied themselves on the way down, survivors left bloody handprints on the walls of the stairwell. It was about this time, while helping the wounded evacuate, that he noticed the acrid smell of cordite hanging over everything.

"I'm covered in blood myself. I didn't realize it for a couple of hours."

***

While that was going on, **William Schooley** told his showering roommate that he and the others were going downstairs.

"All three of us headed out of the suite and down the flight of pink marble stairs to the main lobby. The exit door frames were hanging off the hinges and looked as if someone had grabbed them and twisted them. We made our way out through the rubble and carefully outside.

Broken glass was everywhere, why I still had my shoes on I can't really say as I always took them off when I came home. This was one of the first strange coincidences that happened that night.

Steve and I went out between the buildings, still unsure whether the buildings were safe. We then saw it; about 200 feet high, between the buildings, a huge mushroom shaped blast cloud. I remember it was incredibly light, at the time it didn't register why. Later I realized it was the palm trees outside the perimeter which were on fire."

In the meantime, **Michael Willis** and his group–

"were directed to go outside and gather in the center of the compound. My first thought was that we were making ourselves even more vulnerable and open to another attack. At this point we still didn't know if it was a car bomb, mortar, or Scud missile. Rumors were flying as to what was going on.

An announcement came over the Giant Voice asking for people to help care for the wounded. I remember seeing a very nervous security forces member wearing a helmet, boots, and boxer shorts holding an M-16.

About that time our maintenance superintendent finally arrived. He was the last person unaccounted for in my unit. He had been at our work compound on the other side of the base when the bombing occurred. By the time he got to our barracks, it was empty.

He had started looking to see if anyone was still in the building when he was met by security forces, who ordered him to the ground at gunpoint. Everyone was nervous and on edge and there were rumors that the compound had been breached. The actions of the security forces members was definitely understandable. Once the airman first class realized that he forced a senior master sergeant to drop to the ground, he was quick to apologize and help him up.

This was no ordinary senior master sergeant. He was a former Marine with combat experience in Vietnam. The first class noticed a lot of blood coming from the old Marine's leg and pointed it out, to which the senior said it was just a scratch. I and the other squadron leadership listened to this old Marine's story as he laughed about it. He then asked if anyone had a Leatherman on them.

I handed him mine and he used it to pull about a four-five inch chunk of glass from his upper thigh. He didn't even squint as he pulled the glass out. He wiped the blood on his pants and gave me back the Leatherman."

***

Meanwhile, **Larry Oliver** and his security group began to move up to the bomb site.

"Before departing the LED, I remember the Captain - the 4404(P) SPS[8] Operations Officer - talking about 'Gooks' - I kid you not. Even the Chief was wondering what he was talking about. It was time to go, as I didn't want any part of that conversation.

Along the way, TCNs were challenged, put on the ground and tie-wrapped. I remember seeing one SP in civilian attire with a gash across his thigh. He didn't even realize it himself. We convinced him to sit down and it was at that point he realized the injury and went into a minor state of shock.

I remember moving up to the scene of the attack, looking up at the sky through the shade above the sidewalks to a sky full of refractions in the dust from the flames of burning trees & bushes, flying debris, etc. wondering what hell we were in for when we got there.

As we got on scene, the Captain was right behind us and stated to me 'shoot anyone who comes through the hole in the perimeter.' I recall the other men with me did not agree with the order either, so we did not.

There was a Saudi male running toward us with an AK-47 rifle and in traditional attire. I remember

---

[8] 4404(P) SPS - 4404 is the Wing number, with the (P) standing for provisional, SPS stands for Security Police Squadron. "Provisional" meant "an assemblage of personnel and equipment temporarily organized for a limited period of time for the accomplishment of a specific mission."

this to this day. I did not engage him for two reasons. For one, I did not know how to challenge him in the Arabic language and he was holding the AK-47 in a 'low-ready' position. There are three preconditions to deadly force and they are opportunity, intent and capability. He had the opportunity, the capability, but did not show intent.

I took cover and followed him in my sights to watch his actions. As he got to the site, he shouldered the rifle and began to help. Come to find out, the man with the AK was a Saudi Arabian policeman responding to assist."

***

Back at his own group, **Leighton Reid** and others helped the wounded outside to a volleyball court where they tried to render what first aid they could.

"I was never so proud of – all that training kicked in," he said. "It could have been a lot worse."

A week before the blast, Reid had conducted another briefing for newcomers. At that briefing, a young airman had asked what to do in the case of an attack.

That same young airman now lay bleeding on top of the squadron's picnic table, suffering from a sucking chest wound. Minutes earlier, he had been calmly eating a pizza when he was struck by a hurtling chunk of concrete.

Reid and others relied on their training to try to save him, using a military ID card to try to seal the wound to stop the bleeding.

"I know we lost him. His only crime was being 19 years old."

***

As the magnitude of the disaster sank in, **William Schooley** spoke quietly to himself, *those bastards finally did it.* *After all the beefed-up security and all the briefings.*

"Steve and I stood there each reflecting on his own thoughts, for a few seconds. All those years of training kicked in; Steve turned to me saying, 'Do you have a flashlight? We have to get over there and help.'

We both ran back to our building. In the stairwell were several people bleeding mostly from arms, legs, and faces. One of them I recognized, Young, a line driver from mid-shift. I checked his wounds; they looked bad but were only scratches. He was OK.

Steve took one of the wounded to his room. The injured airman had a glass shard imbedded in his foot. With no first aid kits handy, Steve wound up using one of his bed sheets. The wound left an 18-inch circle of blood in Steve's carpet."

Retrieving his Mini Maglight[9], Schooley headed back downstairs. Wounded from other buildings were coming outside with others helping them get to the clinic. Some carried the wounded on their backs, arms and legs wrapped in blood soaked sheets.

"Looking down I noticed the concrete sidewalk was covered with glass and blood splatters, in some places there were large puddles. At this point the light was gone, the fires must have burned out.

One particular sight that will haunt me forever, a big white weightlifter guy carrying a small black

---

[9] Flashlight

fellow wrapped in a blood-soaked sheet in his arms, heading towards the clinic. Scenes like these were repeated over and over again that night, airmen tending to their fallen comrades.

We took care of each other. We had to."

***

Larry Oliver remembers that shortly after tracking the Saudi policeman, Lieutenant Colonel Traister was on scene. He asked how he and his group were doing.

"We stated that the guys at the scene were okay but we had thought the Captain was not giving lawful orders. We explained to Lieutenant Colonel Traister our concerns, citing his order about shooting people coming through the perimeter. It was at that point he asked the direction the Captain headed and brought an SP with him. I'm not positive about what happened with the Captain, but I believe that resulted in the end of his career."

Then Oliver saw the first body.

"We were posted at the base of Building 131, to the right side in - between the underground parking garage and the remains of Building 131. The first body was brought out on an orange litter and set on the ground right in front of me. I could not understand what I was seeing and thought to myself, why wasn't anyone helping this man? The rescue personnel returned, to my relief, but simply rolled the man out of the litter on the ground. This man had no face or right arm below the elbow.

I covered the body with a piece of cardboard to protect him from the media cameras that had arrived, not to mention the fact I did not want to see that all night. It got to be a little bit of a shoving match between us and the Saudis to keep the body covered. We won.

There was a second body recovered and was put into the back of an ambulance that had recently arrived. I had to ask the SP to see if there was any identification. To this day, I regret that order because I know how it affected him. We speak on occasion and I have apologized on many occasions. Personally, I know how I was affected as a young man in my 20's and how much that must have affected him in addition to the attack itself.

The rest of the night was very fluid: expediting rescue vehicles in and out, attempting to communicate with our Saudi counterparts through language barriers, picking up letters from/to home, pictures of kids and families, etc. We saw almost all of the bodies and body parts recovered from the rubble that night.

At one point I was on the left side of the building next to a line of destroyed vehicles parked alongside the road and looked up at the building. What I saw superimposed an image in my head forever.

There was a window about ¾ of the way up the side of the building. The window was gone and there was an impact mark where someone's head had hit the wall and disintegrated. From the window frame on down the wall was a thick truncating blood flow. I looked to my feet and realized I was standing in gray brain matter. Somehow I did not have the appetite for the water I had come to obtain from the Medics.

Somehow, someway, an SP from Eglin AFB was able to get a message through back stateside that we all survived the attack.

The SP leadership from Eglin was able to contact our families in an expedited manner so they knew we were alive and well.

I simply cannot thank them enough, as this was my worst thought that they'd not know for a while."

***

As that was going on, **William Schooley,** leaving the area of his own building, ran toward the place the cloud from the explosion rose.

"Upon reaching the parking lot I saw a girl about 10 feet from the pavement limping, many cuts visible on her legs. I offered to help her, but she said, 'I'm OK, please go to the building and help the others.'

I saw two uninjured and told them to help her to the clinic. They responded immediately, happy to be able to help in some way.

Having no idea exactly where I was going, other than towards the blast I had seen, I ran to the building on the left of the blast, which was actually the building next to the one seen so many times on television.

I turned on my flashlight and noticed huge strands of barbed wire and glass everywhere. The residents were starting to come out of the building. Many suffered cut feet from the glass on the ground. In their haste they had forgotten to put on shoes.

The sidewalk had several strands of barbed wire across it. I put my light in my mouth and began clearing a pathway. It wasn't until later that I realized this was the perimeter fence. It had come to rest more than 100 feet from where it was originally.

With the pathway cleared I looked up, stretchers were beginning to be brought out of the doorway. I hurried over to the picnic table area, where the wounded on stretchers and doors were being placed on the ground. Someone yelled to clear off the table next to me. I grabbed a piece of metal and began pushing the debris off, someone from the other end upended it and all the glass slid off.

Immediately a litter was placed there, the victim was unconscious. The stretcher bearers ran back into the building. I was alone with him, my vision narrowed, I remember it like looking through a tube. I tried to remember self-aid and buddy care, but could recall nothing to help in this situation.

I examined his wounds, his left arm was almost completely detached, and the torso was sliced open in several locations with large chunks of tissue hanging out. The extent of his injuries were completely beyond my ability to stabilize.

I then realized he was already dead. There was nothing I could do.

I remember thinking to myself – how can this be? A few minutes ago I was watching a movie.

Someone was screaming for the medical corpsmen. There were none. I can remember feeling completely helpless, we had no medical supplies and our training was so limited. There were many others around me who, I'm sure, felt the same way. It's just that you felt so damn helpless and so terribly alone.

The on scene commander, the guy with a radio, was standing on top of a picnic table. He ordered all of us to the Desert Rose, the chow hall. He said, 'Secondary attacks are possible.'

I heard sirens coming – help was on the way. Reasoning that many times the best way to help is to let the professionals do their job, I left for the Desert Rose.

At the Desert Rose, there were probably a couple hundred people standing around. Adam Smith was there, he was not only my airman - he worked for me on mid-shift Control - but a friend. We stood there for a while and discussed our disbelief at what had happened. All the carnage we had seen had such an unreality about it. I believe this was due to our unprepared mental state for such an attack."

***

Aboard the bus where he had met someone from his own town, **John Gaydos** and the other injured were taken to the clinic and the courtyard just outside.

"It was chaos, people everywhere. The doctor was moving from patient to patient trying to see who needed to be immediately evacuated and who could be treated there or wait longer.

The girl who was on the bus had to go help others. I tried to get her to stay but others needed help. I leaned my head up to try to look around but people were everywhere with all sorts of injuries.

When I looked to my right where the desk was for checking into sick call, I saw a female officer. Her eye was dangling from the socket. I saw her hold it up and ask the doctor if it could be saved. He

Through the Perilous Night

took only a moment in his diagnosis and said no from across the room. Even I could see it could not be saved, it was clearly deflated. She began rummaging around in the desk and came out with a pair of black handled scissors like the type for cutting paper. She clipped the eye at the optic nerve and slapped a 4x4 piece of gauze bandage over her eye. She bandaged herself up and then proceeded to check on the injured, myself included.

Maybe a minute or so later the first ambulance arrived. As I was taken to the ambulance I could see what looked like body bags in the court yard. Even to this day I wonder if I really saw them. How could someone have gotten a body bag and gotten them to the clinic so fast?

I was loaded aboard the ambulance along with another young man who was in shock. The nurse in the ambulance tried talking to him and so did I but he never spoke and never blinked that I could see. We were racing down the highway to get to the base hospital when the ambulance began to slow. The driver was telling the passenger in front and the nurse that the road ahead was blocked ahead. Some kind of checkpoint. I thought it was something like terrorists trying to stop us from getting to the hospital.

In my shock I sat up and told the nurse that when we stopped I was going to get out and clear the way, don't stop just get that guy to the hospital. That nurse's eyes got the size of dinner plates and told me to stay where I was. I didn't lay back down till the ambulance was moving again.

At the hospital, I was asked if I could move myself from the gurney to a bed. I slid over on my own. Then a doctor asked what had happened. I said, 'don't you know?' He said, 'No, I was at my sink and the windows blew out. I knew I would be needed so I came here.' He climbed onto my chest and began pulling on my teeth while the staff were wheeling the bed toward surgery. I later learned this was to check for loose teeth so that I would not choke on them during surgery. I still have flashbacks and need a bite block any time a dentist goes into my mouth.

After surgery I woke up in a room with three other guys. The doctor came in to speak to me. He told me he had closed my wounds but that there was not time to reattach my nerves or arteries that were damaged. There was not even enough time to get all of the glass out of my wounds.

He gave me a set of medical records that he placed under my pillow. He told me when I got to the next hospital to let them know and they could clean my wounds and try to fix the damage.

A nurse came in and asked if I needed anything. I jokingly said, 'Yes, I need something for the pain.'

She returned with a needle and a brown bag. She set the bag between my legs on the blanket and stuck me in the thigh with the needle. I didn't wake up again until I was being moved from my bed to a stretcher. My brown bag and medical records followed me.

We were again loaded onto a vehicle and this time taken to a waiting aircraft. I can remember as my stretcher was being walked to the plane there was a line of airmen on either side leading to the aircraft. It made my heart swell with pride and gave me a sense of safety that cannot be put into words."

***

Over in the Desert Rose, **Mike Dunn** started to get anxious.

"I really just need to be out of here. I'm just thinking, how can I help? What can I do instead of just sitting here?"

Hearing an officer use a handheld radio, Dunn thought;

"I'm the POC for the land mobile radios in the region, and there's guys out there that are working on the bomb site right now. With all this radio chatter that's going on, those batteries are going to start going dead."

Dunn convinced officers in charge that he needed to get out of the Desert Rose and set up charging stations. He got a vehicle and some people.

"We went to the base, I had them grab up every battery, every charger they could find."

***

Angel Marsh, whose last memory had been "trying to tap the guy in front of me," recovered consciousness to find herself under medical care.

"I woke up on a gurney. And I had an IV in my arm. I had a neck brace on. And there was some Army chick that I didn't know. She was talking to me, asking me all these questions. Trying to keep me awake. At that point, I still didn't know what happened. She was asking, 'Is there anything I can get for you, or whatever?' I remember asking her if I could have a gun."

A doctor examined her injuries.

"I was all cut up on my arms and my legs. He was concerned about my Achilles, It didn't get sliced, but it got cut. He wanted me to be seen as soon as possible, but obviously I wasn't a life or death situation."

The doctor had Angel put aside with a group to go to a downtown hospital, although she did not know that was the plan at the moment. In addition–

"I don't know how, but I guess I kept my cigarettes in my hand. Because I still had them."

When she learned the group was going to a hospital downtown–

"I was like freaking out because I didn't know who did what to us. For all I knew, it was people right outside the base."

Angel asked a supervisor from her shop to go with her, but he declined. Then she asked a senior airman (E4), who was recording names of who was going where, and he agreed. Angel, the senior airman, and two other wounded were loaded onto an ambulance and sent to the hospital downtown.

"We get there, and people start banging on the ambulance doors in the back. And we're like, uh oh! It ended up being the hospital workers, they were just trying to get us out."

Hospital staff stitched up her Achilles heel injury but she waved off attention to her other injuries. While she was in the waiting room with others, the staff kept wanting to wrap a sheet around her because she was in shorts.

"I kept yelling, I'm hot! Leave me alone!"

About 5 a.m., the group was discharged and a bus took them back to Khobar Towers. Approaching the gate was–

"scarier than getting blown up. You could see the smoke, smell the smells."

***

Back at the Desert Rose, **Trena Schmidt** looked for the other three airmen who had deployed with her. It was there that she first learned the attack was a truck bomb.

Despite the confusion and chaos, she dove into assisting the wounded, survivors with concussions, in shock or airmen who just needed help to calm down. She assisted the medical help by holding IVs and stopping bleeding wounds. She ignored her own cuts on her feet and legs.

"In my eyes, there were people hurt a lot worse. It wasn't long before you could start to hear sirens, ambulances coming and things like that. And then I remember hearing some helicopters coming in… From there, everything's kind of a blur."

Schmidt could not remember going back to her barracks.

***

About 11 p.m., **Leighton Reid** made his way to an Army building across the compound, the only building left with power.

"One of the few working televisions showed that the attack was already breaking on the news," he said. "Not surprising as the blast was heard and seen some 30 miles away in Bahrain and from the Saudi Aramco compound on the other side of the airbase."

Reid asked to use an Army phone to make notifications up his chain of command. In a small notebook he carried, he found a number for the command post at Ramstein Air Force Base in Germany.

When he finally got through to someone, an Air Force Captain told Reid–

"I can't do that, I don't want to wake the commander up" for the urgent report Leighton was trying to make.

"Captain, I highly suggest you wake his ass up," Reid replied. "The President is going on television in a few minutes."

***

After seeing the damage to the building next door, **Scott Wolff** went back to helping the injured.

"I went back to the clinic area - seeing all the injured people, my emotions of what I had just went through and seen, hit me and I had to go be by myself to gather my thoughts.

One of my friends came over and asked if I was all right. I shook my head no. He noticed the blood on my arm and back from my wounds and said I needed to go get checked out.

They had set up additional areas to treat the injured in the dining facility. While me and a friend were waiting to be seen, the breaking news came on the big screen TV about the bombing. I managed to get some levity out of the moment by saying to my friend, 'did you hear about this?'"

***

Larry Oliver's security group was finally relieved about 11 a.m.

"We could not leave our post since there was a huge hole in the perimeter. Try sleeping in 120 degree plus heat with your mind racing after the events of that night. Some of us had to sleep elsewhere since our building, Building 129, was damaged badly by the blast.

Either way, we didn't have A/C or many belongings at all. We were lucky to have a complete uniform."

***

About that same time, **Leighton Reid** and others moved to the chow hall to set up a command post to coordinate disaster response.

"That's when we started doing the casualty count."

It was several hours after the blast that Reid finally made his way to a bathroom and saw himself in the mirror. Then he understood why people had looked at him so strangely. His face was bloody, his ears were bloody, his clothes were soaked in blood. He washed up as best he could, but the only thing he could find to use for bandages for his ears was toilet paper.

"I came out looking like a rabbit."

***

Meanwhile, back at the Desert Rose, **William Schooley** remembers that an Air Force NCO, Chief Whitley asked Schooley to "find the ammo people" and have them all stay at the corner of Building 110, which was right next to the Desert Rose.

"The Ammo guys as usual were more than happy to comply, they put their complete trust in the Chief. We began checking each other for wounds.

Those in need of attention were escorted to the clinic. One of the ammo guys was an EMT. Somewhere in all the chaos he had gotten his hands on a bag full of bandages. He began patching up the more minor injuries among us.

We stayed there for about three hours; the waiting seemed endless as we all sat in silence. Each person trying to make sense of what they had experienced.

The TCNs brought us water and orange juice. I take back all the bitching about the food; these guys were real champs that night. Karen Fanning had the forethought to bring a carton of cigarettes with her. That night, people who had never smoked before in their lives took up the habit."

***

Paralegal **Selena Zuhoski** spent the rest of the evening helping provide first aid to the injured.

"I continued to provide first aid to other gravely wounded individuals, to include an Airman that had multiple shards of glass and other materials sticking out of his neck and leg. I was relieved to hear several days later that he had survived the ordeal. He thanked me for helping him and potentially saving his life. I'm proud of the way that everybody responded.

I think that under the circumstances everybody just kind of acted instinctively.

Nobody really got emotional that night. It wasn't until later on that it kind of hit us. That night everybody just got it done, did what they had to do."

***

Midnight came and went.

Michael Willis–

"It was probably around 1:00 a.m. now and our commander decided we needed to call home to let them know what happened and that we were fine. He picked the two captains, a staff sergeant and me to go to our work compound to make the call. We drove over and started making phone calls. I remember first calling my wife but didn't get an answer. I then called my parents and spoke to my mom.

My only thoughts were that I needed to talk to my wife and let her know that I was safe. I didn't want her to hear about the bombing on the news - CNN International was already reporting it - and wonder if I was still alive.

I remember hearing one of the captains arguing with the commander back home. Once he hung up we got to hear the other side of the conversation. He had been trying to tell the lieutenant colonel that we had been attacked but the lieutenant only wanted to talk about how someone had received a STEP promotion.[10] The last thing the captain said on the phone was, 'Sir, I don't give a damn who got promoted. We have dead airmen here.' Even today I still have a hard time believing that conversation actually happened.

Now our commander made the decision to have everyone come to the work compound since we could not go back to our barracks. I set up a triage

---

[10] Stripes for Exceptional Performers. It is a program to promote exceptional airmen outside of the normal promotion process.

and began looking over all of our troops. I pulled out glass, cleaned wounds, stitched up a couple of wounds, and bandaged up others. All of those Self-Aid and Buddy Care classes really came in handy. We spent the rest of the night there and I don't think anyone slept. There wasn't much talking going on either."

***

At **William Schooley's** group in the Desert Rose:

"About two-thirty we were told to find a place to sleep in Building 110. Adam (one of Schooley's roommates) and I wound up in the Master Sergeant's suite. It was there we saw the news reports on the bombing.

Our major concern was that family members in the States had seen these reports and were hysterical, not knowing the whereabouts or safely of their loved ones. There was a great deal of cursing at CNN that night.

Adam and I decided to go out on the balcony and smoke. The balcony looked down on the Desert Rose, which had become the clinic. We looked directly down on the triage area; the blood was literally running across the pavement to the drain, scattered bandages, and a few stretchers. There were no injured to be seen. They had all been transported to hospitals or were inside the Desert Rose. At this point Adam became extremely upset; the emotional shock was taking a terrible toll on him. He couldn't get over the injured people and destruction he had seen. I spent a great deal of time talking with him that night. Focusing on his problems gave me an opportunity not to think about my own feelings.

We were allowed to return to our own buildings about 4 a.m. Adam, Carol Easily, another Ammo Trooper and I weren't tired, so we walked down to the bombed building. The perimeter was taped off like a crime scene with Security Police standing guard.

We sat on the curb and talked with some of the cops. Many of them were in partial uniforms or civilian clothes, the only identifier their M-16's. They told us many stories.

One of them had been a lookout on top of the bombed building. The only thing that had saved him was he was away checking his mail at the time of the explosion. He told us of the playground on the other side of the fence and the children that were playing there, as well as the destruction to downtown Al Khobar.

He also told us the truck had tried to come on base and was stopped.

I shudder to think of what might have happened if the bombers had gotten through. Additionally, he said the bombers had left their truck and gotten in a car and driven off. For some reason, I think I would have felt better if they would have died in the blast. There might have been some justice in that.

He also said there were reports of three other bombings downtown: the Old Mall, New Mall and a Thai restaurant.

All these places were known to be frequented by Americans."

***

Throughout her ordeal, **Jessica Bradshaw** remembers being wide awake, adrenaline fueling her.

"I was ready to kill anyone who came at us. I wasn't afraid, I wasn't sacred, I was just more angry. But still doing my job."

She was irritated when she found people taking photos of wounded and dead bodies.

"It just felt so disrespectful. It was a very long night. And then it eventually wasn't so tense. It felt like a couple of hours were very tense and then when daylight hit, it wasn't as bad."

Bradshaw got back to her own dorm about 4 or 5 a.m. The night shift had stayed on all night and should have been relieved by then. She and the others were told to get what sleep they could and fall back out by 11 a.m.

After the long night of carnage, morning finally came.

CHAPTER 5
Dawn's Early Light

Photo by SSGT Trena Frazier-Schmidt

In the days that followed, **Mike Dunn** went through some of the damaged buildings to assist with cleanup and to secure communications equipment left behind in the chaos.

"I came upon a couch where you could see someone had been sitting facing the window and the window had blown in. And there were shards of glass all over the couch except for where this person had been sitting. And you could see where they had little triangles of glass that had smudgy, bloody fingerprints on one end. It was them pulling the glass out of themselves as they sat on the couch. They were sitting in a neat pile.

There was a spot where someone had come out, you could see their struggle from their room out to the hallway and then down and out of the stairs. You could see it was a hurt individual. You could see where he hit the wall, you could see where he dripped blood down the banister, down the steps. It made me wonder if that guy, was he okay?

There was a spot of blood, I'd never seen such a big puddle, in the hallway of the building I was in. You could just see that person had come to rest there.

To look at it, and know it was from a comrade, a human being, it was a powerful thing to have to digest in a moment like that. You're still there, you're at that place where this just happened. And you're not leaving soon."

In July, Dunn headed back to the States—

"Going back to a broke home, a busted marriage. When I got to San Antonio, all her stuff was gone and all the baby's stuff was gone."

***

Angel Marsh made a point of finding the airman who had helped her get out of the building and thanking him. He left to go back to the States two days later.

Marsh particularly remembers irritation at media who were allowed on the base. One day she was walking to the Desert Rose to go get some lunch.

"I was limping everywhere I went."

As she was walking, a TV cameraman started filming her without her permission, focusing on her injuries.

"I was trying not to cry. I wasn't sad, I was just mad."

Marsh was supposed to stay until August, but due to her injuries she was sent back to the States shortly after the 4th of July.

***

Through the Perilous Night

Scott Wolff —

"–got seen by one of the medical personnel and got stitched up. Later that night, or early the next morning, we went to the commander's suite and I was able to call my wife to tell her I was okay.

Sometime in the early morning hours we were able to try to get some sleep, when I took off my pants I found glass fragments in my bloused up pants.

We were able to return to Building 130 to retrieve our belongings. In the light of day, we could see all the damage: door blown out of the wall, AC unit blown completely out or hanging out of the wall. I found the recliner I would have been sitting in had I not gone to my room. It was blown across the room in to a couch and the frame was broken. I'm sure I would have been hurt far worse or killed if I had been sitting in it.

For the next few weeks any loud noise made me jump, especially when you would lie down to sleep. I believe it was the next day, after the bombing, me and almost everyone on base went out to the terminal area to watch the 19 flag-draped coffins be loaded on the C5 Galaxy. It was a sad and emotional time.

We stayed in Saudi Arabia for about another month. After a few days off we returned to work. One day I was sitting at my desk when the light went out. I immediately ducked and covered."

***

Paralegal **Selena Zuhoski** stayed until July 11.

"I performed inspections of damaged personal property, conducted claims briefings, processed and paid claims for reimbursement of personal property.

One of things I remember about this is that almost everyone had a boom box to claim and I was required to verify they were damaged. I had a pile of them in the corner of the building we were working out of.

The day after FBI investigators got in country, I was talking to one about how they would go about the investigation. He told me they would try to find as many of the fragments as possible.

He mentioned they used strong magnets as one of the tools to do this. I thought about those boom boxes and mentioned them to the agent. The next day the agent came by my office, collected about 20 boom boxes, which each had two speakers, and used the strong magnets in them to search for metal fragments."

After dealing with so many injured comrades and so much damage, she soon had to deal with her own injury–

"I started having seizures a few weeks later and returned to the states."

***

For **Jessica Bradshaw** and her crew—

"our shifts were crazy."

Sometimes 12 or 16 or 18 hours long. There were extra shifts because they were short-handed, due to the loss of wounded airmen.

Occasionally there were reports of red lasers pointed at people from somewhere off the base. Some people were observed on rooftops near the base.

Army soldiers came on the base to assist the security teams, but—

> "we didn't really know who they were and they weren't armed. So it was like, why do I have to have this guy hanging out with me when he's not even armed?"

An FBI team came, sifting through evidence. "And then TWA 800 went down[11] and all the FBI left for that." Then there were the reporters.

> "The media was crazy. The media – that's what really annoyed me. Sitting in the dining facility, we were watching the funeral on TV, and you couldn't even watch it because the media was right there in your face wanting to know what your reaction was. That infuriated me.
>
> You didn't have time to grieve because you're still working. And then to see President Clinton up on the stage with all the bodies and the coffins and here comes the media, expecting you to cry. It just so pissed me off."

***

Meanwhile, **Dusty Huntley**'s return to his tower had shocked his fellow airmen.

---

[11] Trans World Airlines Flight 800 exploded and crashed into the Atlantic Ocean off the east cost of the United States on July 17, 1996. The cause was never officially determined.

"Upon returning to our dorm, I found everyone cleaning up as much of the glass and debris as possible with whatever light they had found.

I was given an astonishing look and was asked, 'Where have you been? You were listed as missing in action (MIA).' They proceeded to tell me that I needed to call my wife to let her know that I was alright.

Apparently, everyone forgot that I was helping with our wounded, everyone being our First Sergeant and Flight Chief. When I finally got through to Roberta, she was in tears. Apparently, no one from my home base bothered to tell her, she found out from my mother, who had seen on CNN and had called Roberta to see if I was all right."

***

As with the others, work went on for **Michael Willis**, regardless of what they endured.

"In the morning we drove back to Khobar from the flight line and saw the damage. We weren't allowed near Building 131 - ground zero for the truck bomb - but could see it took a beating. Our building was just hit with a shock wave, but it knocked almost every door off of its hinges and knocked in a good number of the air conditioning units. Most of the windows were gone also.

As I walked into my suite, the first thing I saw was the couch I had been sitting on less than 30 minutes before the blast. It had been shoved back about five feet up against the concrete interior wall that separated the day room from my room. Right through the middle of the back of the couch was a piece of glass about three by four feet in size. It had gone through the couch and was imbedded about three inches into that concrete wall.

If it wasn't for a bad movie on the TV, I would not be here today... I see the image of that pane of glass in the wall almost daily."

***

For **William Schooley**—

"The sun was coming up and a terrifying scene was before us. In the daylight the damage was very apparent, with almost all the windows blown out, the sliding glass doors were gone from most suites, and the concrete was stained with blood as if someone had gone crazy with red paint. It all seemed like a distant memory, but the evidence was all around. The entire compound we knew so well seemed to have a surreal quality. Just hours before everything was so normal. The emotional shock was starting to set in.

The three of us (he, Adam and Carol Easily) walked back to our building. All the ammo guys were outside and Chief Whitley was giving a briefing. He told us not to worry about the Dump, the Munitions Area, everything was OK out there, and not to plan on going to work until mid-shift. He also said to get some rest and then to help with the clean-up. In all my years in the Air Force I have never seen sleep put before work. He then dismissed us.

On the way back to my suite, I noticed the phones were unlocked in the lobby. Usually we had to sign out the key, only being allotted one call a week. I thought I should call home. After three tries I finally got through to Munitions Control at Kirtland AFB. I reasoned that they would be the best ones to spread the word to my wife and my shop that I was all right.

    I then went back to my suite on the first floor. Upstairs the destruction was all around.

    The sliding glass doors were in the middle of the living room. The kitchen door was blown in. Most of the windows in the rooms were gone. The front door jamb was pushed out about five inches. The doors between the living room and my suite were so cockeyed they wouldn't close. I found the door latch in the middle of my room. It must have gone flying off during the explosion. The under-pressure that caused all of this must have been tremendous!

    I have spent the last fifteen years of my life working with explosives, but I was truly in awe of the explosive power unleashed here.

    My suite mates and I spent a couple of hours cleaning up the debris. Trying to follow the Chief's instructions, I laid down to get some sleep, but it wouldn't come. I think I was past the point of exhaustion. I could see no reason to just lie there, so I decided to go downstairs. To my surprise; the phones were still open in the lobby. I could only imagine what Missy was thinking back home. Again, after several tries I got through, when I heard her answer the emotions came like a flood. As I relayed what had happened I cried. The horror was too much to keep in.

Afterwards, I went upstairs and slept. I was lucky. Many others couldn't. The memories were too terrible or there was the fear that when they closed their eyes it would happen again."

***

Larry Oliver also remembers the universal exhaustion–

"How we all made it through the night was probably due to sheer adrenalin, anger, spite and a burning desire for payback," he recalled. "By now, I think it was safe to say most of us had been up a good thirty hours with minimal rest if any at all.

The next morning, we were allowed to go back into our original buildings to recover any property we had that was not already destroyed. We could only do this a few at a time, with civil engineer representatives considering the building was so badly damaged. As for where I moved to after the attack and for the remainder of the TDY I honestly have no recollection of that detail. It was another building closer in to the middle of the base, that's all I can recall. Our emphasis was on work and the continued threat and truly, nothing more.

At 1800 that same night, we were back to work on the same post. The Saudis and fellow Americans were sifting through the debris for clues and for personal property of the deceased. I do not recall what night it was, immediately afterward or the following day, but I found someone's wallet. I wanted to give it back to him when I saw him but was later told that he was among those killed. I turned it in for evidence at the LED.

A few days later toward the end of our shift in the morning, there was a bomb threat that was broadcast from the Saudi side to our Coalition side via loudspeaker and our translator. I was at an Entry Control Point on the airbase with another kid I supervised, the one I mentioned earlier in this recollection, and he kind of lost it. I remember us putting on our body armor and my grabbing him by the shirt looking up at him - since he was a little taller - and telling him to pull it together. It is my understanding that about a year later, he separated from the Air Force entirely.

Sometime after the bombing, maybe even the following night, I found a wooden ladder that seemed to be handmade along the perimeter inside the fence on the ground. I did call it in to the LED and subsequently destroyed the ladder. I do not know if there was any significance and to be honest, I didn't care. OSI was angry that I had destroyed the ladder but I did not want to leave it intact for further use that may have led to anything malicious against us.

In hindsight, maybe I thought that since we had TCNs working on the base, I did not want to take the risk that it might be the work of a collaborator. It might as well have been a ladder used by the CE people too, but who knows. All I knew is we were under threat, period."

***

The following days "were a blur" to **Dusty Huntley**.

"We had power back and were boarding up the shattered windows and makeshift doors. Some of us helped sift through the rubble looking for personal effects and any other possible casualties. Our night shift, that we were supposed to go in and relieve that night, was still on duty and they were somewhat in the dark as to what happened.

We resumed operations and were on twelves (12 hours on and 12 off) for a while and that's when tempers started flaring, arguments started."

Being the subordinate NCO, Huntley thought that his senior NCO—

"would have broken it up, but as it turns out, he was a pacifist. Kind of ironic I thought. So I had to be the guy to break them up.

In the weeks to follow, they implemented rules to keep us safe, by moving us into the interior rooms away from the perimeter walls, but that created other issues. The folks who were at work that night didn't understand what we had went through and would slam doors and make loud noises when we were trying to sleep. It didn't take much to make us jump out of our skin or go off on each other.

When Patricia (Goldman) was allowed to return to duty, she kept calling me her 'hero,' others called me that as well, said that I was being put in for a medal. I didn't feel like a hero and I didn't want a medal. I just did what I was taught to do while being scared the whole time. Those 19 dead airmen were the heroes. They paid the ultimate sacrifice.

They brought in a C-5 Galaxy aircraft to take our fallen home during the middle of the night, so I had my whole crew out on the ramp to pay respects as they loaded them. I couldn't do anything but cry. I remember in the weeks following, they had us meet in groups to discuss how we were feeling.

I remember a few that did lash out because they were angry. Me, I wasn't sure how to feel."

Trena Schmidt remembers going back to work the next day on heightened alert as she and the others started 12-hour shifts, getting back to business and cleaning up. She remembers everyone being scared.

"I can't remember a lot of details," she said. "I can't even remember when I was able to make a phone call home to let my parents know I was okay."

Schmidt left the country to go back to Pope Air Force Base about three weeks later.

***

As with the others, **Michael Willis** focused on the tasks at hand.

"The wounded were evacuated, we cleaned up, made repairs, and carried on. I rotated back home in September. But it was a very long three months with the constant threat and fear of another attack.

When I got back home, Khobar Towers was already a distant memory for many people. I was more likely to be asked 'what is Khobar Towers' than anything else when the subject came up. This is still very bothering to me today. How quickly we can forget lives sacrificed.

As the days turned into weeks we learned that the truck with the bomb had tried to come on base. I know if it would have been allowed on, it would have parked in front of my building. The other buildings around mine housed security forces, the fire department, communications, and other high value targets. It was a no-brainer and again, I probably wouldn't be here."

***

On August 8, **Jessica Bradshaw** rotated back stateside, to Holloman Air Force Base.

She got to Holloman well after the wounded had returned. She found her reception somewhat cold, with the attitude that *you're not injured, you're fine, they're the ones that are the heroes.*

"I was kind of treated like, it's no big deal and I should just get over it. I did receive a medal for my actions at Khobar Towers, however instead of it being presented to me, an official handed it to me and told me 'they are giving these out like candy.'"

Airmen coming back were required to meet with a mental health counselor. Jessica and another returnee attended a session with an enlisted mental health technician.

"This NCO made it very clear he would rather be doing anything than talking to us," she said. Asked about nightmares, "I lied, I said no, I'm fine…

But it was just all very nonchalant, like we were wasting his time."

Several survivors commented on the negative behavior they encountered when they returned to the states. Fellow airman who had not been at Khobar Towers might make loud noises, such as slamming doors or suddenly dousing hangar lights, adding to their trauma.

***

John Gaydos, who had been so proud to see a line of airmen on either side leading to the aircraft that took him to Germany, also remarked on the negative attitudes he encountered after leaving Saudi Arabia.

> "Where the Saudi hospital had fawned on us giving us our requests, the Army hospital at Landstuhl was all business. They denied even simple requests like water for a thirsty person. I was wheeled to surgery within an hour of arriving.
>
> After surgery the doctors spoke to me. I was told that my artery in my left arm was too damaged to reattach. The nerve was attached but may or may not grow back. I was told if it was not better in six months, then it would never heal. The doctors did not have time to work on my leg. The doctor said that, by the notes in Saudi, that it should heal up. He said that when I got to the U.S., doctors would have to cut it open again, extract the glass and repair the muscle. He said the good news was I would walk again, the bad news was that it would take me a year to learn to walk again."

Later, at Shaw Air Force Base in South Carolina, a doctor briefly stopped to check on Gaydos on a Friday night.

> "An hour or so later the pain in my leg was so bad I called the nurse. I asked when the doctor would be back because I needed something for the pain. I was informed he went home for the weekend and would not be back till Monday morning. I told her I needed something for the pain and was told only the doctor could prescribe that and he would see me on Monday. She left with a smile.

I asked my wife for my brown paper bag that had made the trip. Inside I had enough Vicodin and morphine to numb the base of a week. I took out some pills and the nurse watching from a video monitor came running back in. She told me I could not take them. I told her to tell the doctor on Monday.

Upon my release from the hospital my left arm was in a cast. I was told not to remove the cast until I could be seen at Fort Gordon a nearby Army hospital. They said my arm needed to be seen by a specialist so I didn't have permanent nerve damage. Three months later I took the cast off because it was causing a 'Dupuytren's Contracture.' Now 24 years later I still haven't been seen by that specialist, and I still can't feel with that hand."

CHAPTER 6
Twilight's Last Gleaming

As survivors and mourners dealt with the wreckage, the quest for answers began. Investigations by the Department of Defense (DoD), CIA, FBI, the Air Force and the Saudis commenced.

Among other issues, investigators sought to determine both who was behind the attack and whether adequate security had been in place. In both subjects, politics dominated.

Of the several official reports and investigations, a few stand out: An inquiry commissioned by Secretary of Defense William Perry and headed by retired Army General Wayne Downing; reports by Perry himself; an indictment filed in 2001 based on the FBI investigation; and lawsuits by the families of the victims.

The Downing Report

Three days after the bombing, Secretary Perry appointed General Downing to head "an assessment of the facts and circumstances surrounding the tragedy to give me a fast, unvarnished and independent look at what happened there and offer ideas on how we can try to prevent such a tragedy in the future." At this time, Perry asserted that "The Department of Defense (DoD) knows neither who the perpetrators of this attack are, nor who sponsored them."[12]

---

[12] Perry, W. J. (1996). *Report to the President and Congress on the protection of U.S. Forces deployed abroad* (United States, Department of Defense, Secretary of Defense). Washington, D.C.: Office of the Secretary of Defense

Downing provided his report August 30.

In his Executive Summary, Downing placed the blame squarely on the local commander, Brigadier General Terry Schwalier, and his supervision up to the level of Central Command:

> "The chain of command of the 4404th Wing (Provisional) did not take all measures possible to protect the forces at Khobar Towers. The command relationships established in the region did not support unity of effort in force protection. There were no force protection or training standards provided by U.S. Central Command to forces assigned or deploying to the theater. The rotation and manning policies established by the U.S. Air Force did not support complete, cohesive units, especially Security Police, who were capable of coping with a viable terrorist threat. The Commander, 4404th Wing (Provisional) focused the force protection efforts of the command on preventing a bomb from penetrating the compound at Khobar Towers. Other vulnerabilities were not addressed adequately. Intelligence indicated that Khobar Towers was a potential terrorist target, and incidents from April through June 1996 reflected possible surveillance of the facility. Combined with the November 1995 attack in Riyadh, this should have triggered enhanced force protection measures, regardless of their impact on workload or quality of life. The 4404th Wing commander was ill-served by the intelligence arrangement within his command which focused almost exclusively on the air threat for Operation SOUTHERN WATCH. His senior headquarters, U.S. Air Forces Central Command and U.S. Central Command, did not provide

sufficient guidance, assistance, and oversight to the 4404th Wing (Provisional) to avert or mitigate the attack on Khobar Towers."

Among Downing's findings and recommendations, he concluded that:

- More priority should have been given to paying for security measures,
- Intelligence organizations had provided warning of a potential terrorist attack, although "[t]he ability of the theater and national intelligence community to conduct in-depth, long term analysis of trends, intentions and capabilities of terrorists is deficient,"
- "[F]ield units had limited access" to intelligence,
- "The Commander, 4404th Wing (Provisional) did not adequately protect his forces from a terrorist attack," and
- "Funding for force protection requirements was not given a high priority by the 4404th Wing (Provisional)" (i.e. Brigadier General Schwalier)

Limiting Blame

In 1997, Perry's successor, William S. Cohen, followed up with another report "to assess issues of personal accountability for force protection."[13] This report again placed blame squarely on the shoulders of the local commander: "Brigadier General Terry Schwalier,

---

[13] Cohen, W.S. (1997). Personal Accountability for Force Protection at Khobar Towers (United States, Department of Defense). Washington, D.C.: Office of the Secretary of Defense.

Commander of the 4404th Wing ... recognized that a car or truck bomb parked at the perimeter of the Khobar Towers compound, where many of his forces were housed, represented one of the most serious threats facing his command. He did not, however, take adequate account of the implications of this threat or develop an effective plan for how his command should respond to it."

After listing various measures not taken, such as the absence of an adequate system to warn of an imminent attack, Cohen went a step further. He not only assigned blame to Schwalier, he exonerated everyone above Schwalier – which would include not only the Air Force, but Perry himself as well as the White House: "He (Schwalier) never referred any force protection problems -- including those discussed above -- to his seniors. If he believed that he needed further assistance to implement additional force protection measures, he could have requested it. He did not do so. *That failure should not be imputed to all above him in the chain of command. I have therefore concluded that no adverse action should be taken against those senior to Brig Gen Schwalier in the chain of command* (emphasis added)."

Cohen recommended that Schwalier's name be "removed from the list of those to be promoted" to the grade of Major General.

Survivor William Schooley, now president and co-founder of the Khobar Towers Bombing Survivors Association, found the Downing and Cohen reports more than hard to swallow.

"(President) Bill Clinton chose to vilify Brigadier General Schwalier as his strategy," William said in reviewing the report. "It would absolve him of blame, it would also absolve the intelligence community and the State Department as well.

"Brigadier General Schwalier was the first commander of the 4404th Wing to have a tour of one year, previously the commanders' tours were three months. Schwalier was extremely proactive in tightening security at Khobar Towers."

In particular Schooley remembers that both Schwalier and Traister completed 130 upgrades to security including:

- serpentine barricades – a layout of concrete barriers to force drivers to weave back and forth, preventing a straight line to the entrance of the base;

- roof top look-out posts;

- machine gun nests at the entrance;

- a "rolling barricade" of two large trucks with machine guns in the back;

- and 100% ID checks at the gates with a thorough vehicle search.

Schooley said two of the recommended security upgrades were not completed, the Giant Voice (a speaker system which broadcast to the entire compound) hadn't been used since the Gulf War, and evacuation drills only met the fire marshal's eight-minute requirement. Also, he said, there was no funding for Mylar or protective sheeting on the windows.

Notably absent from the Downing and Cohen reports was precise identification of the attackers. The FBI took the lead in that.

FBI Investigation

More than 250 FBI agents were involved in the investigation of the attack.[14] Based on their investigation, in June of 2001, almost five years after the attack, a federal grand jury in Alexandria, Virginia, indicted 13 members of the pro-Iran Saudi Hizballah group, and one member of Lebanese Hizballah, for the attack.

Nine of the 14 faced 46 separate criminal counts, including conspiracy to kill Americans and employees of the United States, use of weapons of mass destruction, and destruction of U.S. property bombing and murder. The other five were charged with five conspiracy counts.

Although the FBI alleged the attackers had relationships with members of the Iranian government, no Iranians were charged. This was despite the FBI finding that an Iranian military officer had ordered the conspirators—

"to conduct surveillance on the Red Sea coast of Saudi Arabia for sites of possible future attacks against Americans" and that "the attack would serve Iran by driving the Americans from the Gulf region."

Many of the FBI's findings were detailed in its June 21, 2001, public statement detailing the indictment:[15]

---

[14] Schooley et al v. Islamic Republic of Iran et al (District Court, District of Columbia June 27, 2019). MEMORANDUM OPINION by Beryl A. Howell, Chief Judge.

[15] FBI News Release, "Terrorism Charges Have Been Brought Against 13 Members of the Pro-Iran Saudi Hizballah ," June 21, 2001.

The indictment traces the carefully organized bomb plot back to on or about 1993 when Al-Mughassil, under Saudi Hizballah leader Al-Nasser, was head of the "military wing" of the Saudi Hizballah. It is alleged that, at that time, Al-Mughassil was in charge of directing terrorist attacks against Americans and American interests in Saudi Arabia.

Al-Mughassil instructed defendants Al-Qassab, Al-Yacoub and AlHouri, later joined by Al-Sayegh, to begin surveillance of Americans in Saudi Arabia. This operation produced reports that were provided to Al-Mughassil, Al-Nasser and officials in Iran. Al-Mughassil carefully reviewed the surveillance reports, according to the indictment.

During the same time, Al-Jarash and Al-Marhoun conducted surveillance of other sites where Americans lived, worked or frequented, including the U.S. Embassy in Riyadh and a fish market nearby, according to the charges. Later, in early 1994, Al-Qassab began surveillance of locations in the Eastern Province of Saudi Arabia, an area which includes Khobar.

Reports of this operation were provided to Al-Nasser and to Iranian officials, the indictment alleges. In the Fall of 1994, defendants Al-Marhoun, Ramadan and Al-Mu'alem began watching American sites in Eastern Saudi Arabia at Al-Mughassil's direction, and Al-Bahar looked at other sites at the direction of an Iranian military officer, according to the indictment. It was during this time that Al-Marhoun, Ramadan and Al-Mu'alem determined Khobar Towers to be an important American military location and began an effort in the region to locate a storage site for explosives.

In 1995, an Iranian military officer directed Al-Bahar and Al-Sayegh to conduct surveillance on the Red Sea coast of Saudi Arabia for sites of possible future attacks against Americans. During this time, Al-Mughassil told Al-Marhoun during a live-fire practice drill in Lebanon that he enjoyed close ties to Iranian officials who were providing financial support to the party, according to the indictment. Al-Mughassil then gave Al-Marhoun $2,000 in U.S. currency to support continued efforts to identify American sites.

The indictment alleges that it was in or about June 1995 that Al-Marhoun, Al-Ramadan and Al-Mu'alem began regular surveillance of Khobar Towers, at the direction of Al-Mughassil. By late Fall 1995, the three learned that Al-Mughassil had decided that Hizballah would attack Khobar Towers with a tanker truck loaded with explosives.

In early 1996, Al-Mughassil instructed Al-Marhoun to find places to hide explosives, and in February Ramadan drove a car loaded with explosives from Beirut, Lebanon, to the city of Qatif in the Eastern Province of Saudi Arabia, the indictment alleges.

In March 1996, Al-Alawe attempted to drive another explosives-filled car from Lebanon to Saudi Arabia, but he was searched at the Saudi border and arrested. Follow-up Saudi investigation led to the arrests of Al-Marhoun, Al-Mu'alem and Ramadan in April 1996.

Meanwhile, according to the indictment, Al-Mughassil continued planning for the Khobar attack and sought replacements for those arrested. Joining Al-Mughis, Al-Mughassil formed a team consisting of Al-Jarash, Al-Houri, Al-Sayegh and a Lebanese Hizballah member. During this time in 1996, Al-Houri and Al-Mughis began to hide explosives around the Khobar area.

In early June 1996, according to the indictment, a tanker truck was purchased by the conspirators, who then spent two weeks converting the truck into a truck bomb. The group consisted of Al-Mughassil, Al-Houri, Al-Sayegh, Al-Qassab and John Doe (note – an unidentified Lebanese), assisted by Al-Mughis and Al-Jarash. The indictment alleges that Al-Mughassil discussed a plan at this time to bomb the U.S. consulate at nearby Dhahran.

During the first half of June 1996, Al-Mughassil, Al-Houri, Al-Yacoub, Al-Sayegh, Al-Qassab and Saudi Hizballah leader Al-Nasser discussed the planned bombing. Al-Nasser confirmed that Al-Mughassil was in charge of the Khobar attack, according to the indictment.

The indictment details the attack as follows:

- On the evening of June 25, 1996, Al-Mughassil, Al-Houri, Al-Sayegh, Al-Qassab, Al-Jarash and Al-Mughis finalized plans for the attack that night.

- Shortly before 10 p.m., Al-Sayegh drove a Datsun, with Al-Jarash as his passenger, as a scout vehicle into the public parking lot in the front of Khobar Towers Building 131. Behind them was the getaway car, a white Chevrolet Caprice that Al-Mughis had borrowed.

- When the Datsun signaled that all was clear by blinking its lights, the bomb truck, driven by Al-Mughassil and with Al-Houri as a passenger, entered the lot and backed up against a fence in front of Building 131[16].

---

[16] "Sgt. Alfredo R. Guerrero of the Air Force, who was standing guard on the roof, spotted the truck and ordered the building evacuated, a step that is believed to have saved many lives. When the bomb went

- Al-Mughassil and Al-Houri then exited the truck and entered the back seat of the Caprice for the getaway, driving away followed by the Datsun. In minutes the blast devastated the north side of the building. [17]

It would be lawsuits that would finally attempt to hold Iran to account.

In 2002, the District Court of the District of Columbia consolidated lawsuits by the estate of bombing victim Michael Heiser and 16 other victims' families and estates. The suits aimed to hold Iran responsible for the attacks. In deciding the case, the court frequently cited Blais v. Islamic Republic of Iran, another suit by a surviving family.

Altogether the plaintiffs sought, among other results:

---

off, the huge explosion tore the face off the building and rattled windows miles away."

Saudi Arabia Said to Arrest Suspect in 1996 Khobar Towers Bombing. (2015, July 26). *New York Times*. https://www.nytimes.com/2015/08/27/world/middleeast/saudia-arabia-arrests-suspect-khobar-towers-bombing.html

[17] There were at least two estimates of the amount of explosive used.

- The Downing report said the bomb was "the equivalent of 3,000 to 8,000 pounds of TNT."
- The FBI said it was "at least 5,000 pounds of plastic explosives … Comparable to 20,000 pounds of TNT." (FBI News Release, "Terrorism Charges Have Been Brought Against 13 Members of the Pro-Iran Saudi Hizballah ," June 21, 2001).

- Damages for wrongful death and intentional infliction of emotional distress
- Punitive damages of $500,000,000
- Reasonable costs, expenses and attorneys' fees
- Compensatory damages against all defendants in the amount of $3,660,000,000 "plus economic damages in an amount to be determined at trial for each of Decedents' Estates"[18]

The defendants in the case were the Iranian Ministry of Information and Security ("MOIS"), the Iranian Islamic Revolutionary Guard Corp ("IRGC" or "the Pasdaran"), and the unidentified Lebanese, John Doe. ("John Doe" was later dropped when the plaintiffs decided it was unlikely they could identify him.)

The Court ultimately decided the case in December 2006. Among the court's Findings of Fact:

- "...the IRGC is a non-traditional instrumentality of Iran. It is the military arm of a kind of shadow government answering directly to the Ayatollah and the mullahs who hold power in Iran. It is similar to the Nazi party's SA organization prior to World War II. The IRGC actively supports terrorism as a means of protecting the Islamic revolution that brought the Ayatollah to power in Iran in 1979."
- "The attack was carried out by individuals recruited principally by a senior official of the

---

[18] Heiser et al v. Islamic Republic of Iran et al, 466 F. Supp. 2d 229 (District Court, District of Columbia December 22, 2006). MEMORANDUM OPINION by Royce C. Lamberth, District Judge.

IRGC, Brigadier General Ahmed Sharifi. Sharifi, who was the operational commander, planned the operation and recruited individuals for the operation at the Iranian embassy in Damascus, Syria. He provided the passports, the paperwork, and the funds for the individuals who carried out the attack."

- "The terrorist attack on the Khobar Towers was approved by Ayatollah Khameini, the Supreme leader of Iran at the time. It was also approved and supported by the Iranian Minister of Intelligence and Security ('MOIS') at the time, Ali Fallahian…"

- "… the FBI also obtained a great deal of information … from interviews with six admitted members of the Saudi Hezbollah organization, who were arrested by the Saudis shortly after the bombing. These six individuals admitted to the FBI their complicity in the attack on the Khobar Towers, and admitted that senior officials in the Iranian government provided them with funding, planning, training, sponsorship, and travel necessary to carry out the attack on the Khobar Towers. The six individuals also indicated that the selection of the target and the authorization to proceed was done collectively by Iran, MOIS, and IRGC, though the actual preparation and carrying out of the attack was done by the IRGC."

Based on the evidence and findings, the court found in favor of the plaintiffs and awarded various damages to the surviving families. The defendants never showed up in court.

Thirteen years later, in 2019, survivors won another courtroom victory. In William M. Schooley et al versus Islamic republic of Iran et al, the U.S. District Court for the District of Columbia concluded: "Due to their support for Saudi Hezbollah's bombing of the Khobar Towers on June 25, 1996, the defendants are jointly and severally liable for the pain and suffering inflicted on the 101 service member plaintiffs present at Khobar Towers at the time of the bombing, and the emotional distress inflicted on the 118 family member plaintiffs."

In total, the court awarded damages of $892,750,000.

The Highest Levels of Government

William Schooley has not held back in his opinion of how officials dealt with the attack and its aftermath.

"The fact that Iran was behind the Khobar Towers Bombing is indisputable," he said. "But the motives and actions of President Bill Clinton were at best self-centered.

Bill Clinton had three issues to contend with after the bombing: appease Saudi Arabia; an election only four months away; and his desire to quell any talk of military action on the part of the United States.

One, the Saudi Arabians did not see the Khobar Towers Bombing as a significant event. They believed it was an internal matter that only involved them. Why was it important to appease the Saudis? In short, money. Saudi Arabia produces nothing other than oil, which leads to a great deal of wealth.

Two, Clinton's re-election was in danger. After the bombing, he was polling at 40 percent. After his speech at the memorial for the bombing victims, his poll numbers went to over 50 percent.

Three, if Clinton had proposed military intervention at the United Nations, surely it would not be approved.

Even, for the sake of argument, if it had been approved and we had gone to war with Iran, Iraq would have come to Iran's aid. Remember in this time Sadam Husain was still alive and very much in power, he also had the third largest army on the planet. This would cause extreme instability in the Middle East, possibly pulling in other Muslim nations as well. Surely this would not sit well with the Saudi Arabian government and would put our already tenuous alliance in jeopardy.

Additionally, should we have produced 'Shock and Awe' and taken Iran quickly, what was the United States going to with a country that had a fundamental Muslim population?"

To manage the political fallout, Clinton chose, in Schooley's view, to assign guilt.

"Bill Clinton chose to vilify Brigadier General Schwalier as his strategy," Schooley said. "It would absolve him of blame, it would also absolve the intelligence community and the State Department as well. He could make several speeches and waggle his finger talking about justice. That might improve his poll numbers. This would also absolve our best allies in the region.

"The vilification of Brigadier General Schwalier was a tragedy approaching the injustice of the bombing itself. Within a day after the bombing, while the survivors of the bombing were still digging the fallen from the rubble and the wounded were still being treated, Special Forces General Downing was sent to Khobar Towers with one goal in mind: To absolutely destroy Brigadier General Schwalier, blaming him entirely for the bombing."

Those Left Behind

While the defendants never showed up in court, family survivors did. Their testimony, as noted under the heading "Pain and Suffering Damages" in a Memorandum to the Heiser case, spoke volumes of grief.[19] Many family and friends suffered. A few representative examples of their grief are offered here. Out of consideration for the families, names have been omitted. *Bracketing is reproduced as seen in the source document. Where parentheses are used, author has removed names.*

For example, Dr. Dana Cable, an expert witness, licensed psychologist, certified death educator and grief therapist, testified that one victim's mother—

> "has dedicated much of her life to being an advocate for victims of terrorism. She has contacted congressmen about terrorism issues, has attempted to change the laws to protect United States service members, and has tried to place terrorism on the agendas of politicians. She has also spent a great deal of time reading and educating herself about terrorism.
>
> (His father) will move on with his life, but the grief will always be there. Part of that will always be also seeing the pain his wife is going through."

Cable testified on a number of other cases as well,

---

[19] Heiser et al v. Islamic Republic of Iran et al, 466 F. Supp. 2d 229 (District Court, District of Columbia December 22, 2006). MEMORANDUM OPINION by Royce C. Lamberth, District Judge.

noting that another victim's mother—

"has still got a room almost as a museum [which] shows that she is frozen in time at a point back where this happened ... Her pain will continue for quite a period of time."

The mother of another victim said:

"I was devastated. You finally get to sleep; it takes days. You wake up in the morning and it's the first thing you thought of. When you went to bed at night, it's the last thing you thought of . . . And it was hard. ... Music was no longer important to me. I always had music on in the home. It was hard to pick up a book and read. It took quite a while before I could get things together ... but it's always there. There's a pain in your chest that never goes away."

Dr. Cable testified that the son of another casualty—

"lost not only his father, but his best friend and his real support system. So there is a deep sense of loss and loneliness for him. He will continue in grief. Those significant markers down the road are going to be real trial times for him. Just as he indicated, 'Dad wasn't there for my high school graduation.'"

The father of another fatality "just shut down," according to the memorandum.

"He shut himself up in a room in his house and spent time on the computer and away from everyone else. 'I couldn't talk to my wife because if I talked to my wife, she'd cry or if she talked to me I'd cry. I just had a real difficult time (he said).'

According to Dr. Cable, (the father) is in extreme loss and loneliness. He is also having volatile emotions. I think the real difficulty for him, in terms of his loss and loneliness, he doesn't want to get better. He is very lonely. He is very bitter. He is withdrawn from all of those people who could support him, all of those people who love him. . . . [His prognosis is] really very poor . . . His grief will last a lifetime. He doesn't want to forget. He doesn't want to let go of the pain, and I fear will permanently damage any family relationships."

One casualty's wife had known him since she was 14 and he was 16.

"In the weeks after [he] was killed, [she] was very angry. She did not want to eat. Her mother would make her eat by placing a plate of food in front of her and refusing to allow her to leave the table until she ate. [She] could not sleep but she still wanted to be in bed all the time ...

As Dr. Cable testified, she 'is in loss and loneliness ... She has tried to rebuild her life. She has tried to go on ... She still thinks about [him] all the time, and that will never change ... When someone so close to you dies at 18, your new husband ... you worry about everybody else close to you. What if something happened to them, too? She has had to grow up very fast, and that's been difficult. And there will always be those questions of the life we should have had together; all the plans we had and all the promise. That will never fade. That will always stay present."

For a year after the death of another casualty his mother "went to the cemetery every week, and after that at least once a month. She still goes to visit once every other month."

"[She] and many members of her family have attended virtually every memorial service held in Florida, Virginia, and Washington after 1996. There are many memorials in Long Island for him, and the family itself set up a scholarship at (his) college.

[His] mother was not able to return to work until the late summer 1996. Even then, it was very hard for her. She thinks about her son every day. During the last years, September 11, the bombing of the USS Cole, and other terrorist attacks are difficult for her. They bring back all of her terrible memories and make her relive [his] death."

According to Cable, the mother of another fatality:

"is in loss and loneliness ... The loss and loneliness is very deep because of the extreme closeness of the relationship she had with her son. They were a team for a lot of years in there, and that makes it very difficult ... Her grief will continue for the foreseeable future."

The father of another of the victims, said:

"[Our son's] death has ruined my entire family.

My life has changed dramatically since [his] death. If [he] were alive, he wouldn't let me sit around like I do. He never let me sit down ... We miss [him] all the time, every day. Some days are harder than others. We miss him terribly on his birthday and on certain days because he loved his mother's potato salad ... I miss just seeing [him] and talking to him. He always used to drive by the house. It's hard to laugh now or have any fun. It's difficult when my wife and I run into his classmates on the street or in a store. We hardly eat or sleep. I used to be a lot more outgoing. My wife and I used to be more social before [his] death."

Another victims widow:

"is in loss and loneliness. Her loss and loneliness includes this issue of future plans, particularly this having a child together, which creates a real sense of emptiness that they were not able to do that and that that can never be fulfilled. And also loss and loneliness not just for herself, but the impact this has had on her children, because it's had a dramatic impact on them. So she has her own pain for her loss, but her pain for her children as well ... She will ... also experience significant grief into the future. She has not been able to move off of this 'what if?'

According to Dr. Cable, (the brother of one of the casualties) is still in loss and loneliness. He was greatly affected by [his brother's] death. He is able to move on to a degree because of his family, his new family. But I, think that description he uses of a roller coaster is very accurate, that it's still a lot of ups and downs for him.

There is not a sense of real stability. There is still a lot of pain, still a lot of emotion there. Again, for him, it's hard to see - it's hard for him to understand how they could come through so much only to have [his brother] die this way ... He will continue with his grief, more in the sense of waves, because his family will help stabilize his grief to a degree. But there will still be those events and those activities and time when he is going to be kind of overcome for a period with ongoing grief."

Similarly, another victim's mother:

"is still really in loss and loneliness. She still has a hard time admitting to his death. Her prognosis is she is one who does cope but it's very difficult. I (i.e. Dr. Cable) would see her continuing to experience pain, feelings of emptiness for a considerable period of time in the future."

Another victim's mother:

"is still in loss and loneliness, but, she has made conscious efforts to try to move on ... She will continue with her grief. She was a mother for whom the mother role was very important." His father "is still in loss and loneliness. He can't seem to let go; holding on to those memories. The dreams are a part of those ongoing memories. He just can't seem to move to the next step along the way ... His grief will continue."

The mother of another fatality said in an affidavit to the court:

"I feel like my life has not been worth anything since [his] death.

It doesn't matter what you do or how much money you have or how many good jobs you have, there's just a big chunk missing. A part of my life is gone. [He] is gone. Half of our world is gone. I'll never see him again, I'll never see his kids, I'll never know who his wife was, nothing. It stopped. But I can't move on, I'm just there.

I drive by his grave every morning going to work and I drive by on my way home. Even though we try to go on with our lives and be there for our grandson, until I die, I just feel like it's another day. I realize that my life could be worse and I have much to be grateful for, like my material possessions, but it doesn't matter if I lived in the White House or if I lived in a trailer in Alabama, my son is gone. This pain is going to be with me forever, regardless."

The widow of one victim told the court:

"I don't have the self-confidence I used to have. I'm not married. I don't have children. It's difficult and it's just hard. There are certain things I can't do. I don't want people in my home. I used to be social. [I'm] just a lot more closed off than I used to be. I'm not the same person that I was."

One widow of told the court about their son, who was two months old when his father died.

"We were coming back from school and I think they had this thing where the fathers come in and my poor baby said, while we were driving back home, 'I wish I had a daddy, too, just like the other kids.' That really just broke my heart.

What do you say to a seven-year-old that misses something that he didn't even have but for a short period of time? When you go to functions and there's the mother and the father, that's when he gets kind of like he wishes he had both."

One Family's Story:

A more detailed focus on one family's story exemplifies the widening circles of the damage caused by the blast.

Airman First Class Joseph Rimkus was one of the 19 Airmen who died. Rimkus' mother, Bridget Brooks, remembers her first-born as a 6'4" "stringbean" who was determined to enter the military early on.

When he was 11 years old, at the funeral of his grandfather, also named Joseph, young Joseph asked his mother why there was a flag on the coffin.

"Joseph asked me, 'Why does he have a flag on his coffin?' I said, 'Because he served in the military.' And Joseph said, 'I'm going to do it.' So he did.

He was just one of those people that believed in God and believed in men and believed in his country and he was so proud to serve.

He always wanted to be in the military. When he was 17, he wanted to join the military and I wouldn't sign the papers. I told him, 'you might be ready, but I'm not!' Two years later, he didn't need my permission and he did sign up for the military, and he joined.

And he said, 'Mom, now I can have a flag on my casket.' A year later, he did."

In his last letter Joseph had written to his mother—

"He said, 'Mom, there's something going on here. I have so much to tell you, but I won't be able to tell you until I get home.'"

When the attack happened—

"It was nighttime there but it was daytime here. My sister had heard about a bombing in Saudi Arabia and she knew Joseph was TDY there for his first TDY. She was visiting my parents' house and she gave me a call and said, 'Hey, I'm up at Mom's, maybe you can come up and visit. That's all she said. Nothing else. It was very pleasant.

And I had such a feeling of foreboding. It was the strangest feeling. I almost felt like everything I needed to know was given to me right then.

I didn't even call her back. I went outside and my husband had the hood of the truck up and bent down in it. I said, 'Don, I've got to tell you, I can't get over this horrible feeling I have, I've never had this feeling that something bad really happened.'

He stood up and said, 'Bridget, I have to tell you there was a bombing today. But don't worry, it wasn't where Joseph is.' However, Don had misunderstood the location of the attack."

Recalling her sister's seemingly unrelated phone call, Bridget said:

"From that second that I heard her voice on the phone, I knew Joseph had been killed."

Friends and family tried to comfort her that night, telling her that surely her son was safe. Somehow, she knew differently.

"It was like he was right there with me with his arms around me saying, 'Mom, it's going to be OK but I'm in heaven. I was taken."

While waiting tensely for word of her son, Bridget went back to her job as a military analyst at Eglin Air Force Base in Florida. She called a phone number set up for families to ask about their relatives. An officer told her that her son's "status was open," which did not really answer her question. Later she was to learn this meant that the remains of those killed had not been identified.

Bridget went to her mother's home to wait for word.

"Finally one of my friends said, 'Bridget, you only have to worry if they come to you in a group of uniforms. Until you see uniforms coming in a group, and one of them is a chaplain, you do not have to worry.'"

At her mother's, Bridget was in a front room near a window when—

"all of a sudden I looked out the window, and I didn't see heads, I didn't see feet, I just saw the bodies of uniforms in a group coming up the steps."

One of them was a chaplain.

"We stood in a circle and I remember it just burst out of my mouth, the Lord giveth, the Lord taketh away. Blessed be the name of the Lord."

After the bombing Bridget met regularly with a small group of survivors and family members:

"a group of people that you bonded with and held on to.
The boys' squadron commander's wife, and the boys' wing commander's wife, invited the family members in the local area to meet with them to help in any way they could. And boy did they!
All of us would meet and we became so close that one day we're chatting online and (someone) said, 'do you have a name for your group?' We were under pressure to come up with a name so that was our name. Under Pressure."

In her heart, Bridget has felt honored to "carry the flag for the boys after they were killed," bringing passion to her work for the Air Force, and so did the others. One became a member of the FBI and later the Secret Service. Another began working for the Tragedy Assistance Program (TAPS), for Survivors. Bridget was also blessed with several Air Force level awards.

Joseph was Ed Bradley's godson and first grandchild among his family of 10 brothers and sisters. Ed's wife, Dari Bradley, recalls first learning of the bombing over the radio when she was returning to Florida from a doctor's appointment in Alabama.

"My heart sank, nah, it couldn't be Joseph. He is surely somewhere else. I said a quick prayer for him and for all our soldiers. And then a phone call from Ed's mother when I got home. She told me there was a bombing in Saudi Arabia and Joseph was missing.

"I hung up and called Ed at work to tell him. Ed said 'He's dead.' I implored him to not be so negative, suggesting the possibility was just missing, maybe he was just around town and somewhere else." Nearly a week passed before the family finally got the word Joseph was one of the 19 who had died."

Dari remembers Rimkus' mother, Bridget, telling her about a dream she had the night before the bombing.

"Bridget dreamed about Joseph and his brother James as children, playing in military uniforms. Joseph dressed in an Air Force uniform, James in a Navy one. They were playing together happily when suddenly Joseph disappeared and James was left to play all by himself. James said Joseph wasn't coming back.

This dream concerned Bridget very much but her fears were relieved when Joseph called from Saudi Arabia. When she spoke to Joseph, everything was fine; he told her he'd sent her a worry stone. Joseph sensed she was worried about him. He was coming home the next day and was insistent that she locate the gift from a package he'd already mailed to her. After the bombing, Bridget was never without the worry stone and carried it with her always.

Their conversation took place just a mere 12 hours before the bombing ... Their last words were 'I love you.'"

About 40 family members attended the June 30 service at Eglin Air Force Base. At first they were told they would meet with President Clinton, who would also be at the service, then they were told to cut the number of family members to six. Rimkus' stepfather Don declared that either the entire family would meet the president or none of them would. Officials relented.

The morning of the service, Dari awoke from a dream in which her nephew—

"told me to go get his picture that he had just given me at Thanksgiving. Just get it and take it and get President Clinton to sign it."

Dari remembers the reception after the service as being "really strange."

"We're all there, we're all at the reception, and no one is saying a word. You could have heard a pin drop.

And then finally, all of a sudden, it was my decision - I know it's because God made me do it - I got up with Joseph's picture and walked up to General (John) Shalikashvili (Chairman of the Joint Chiefs) and I told him who I was and that I would be very proud if he would sign Joseph's picture for Bridget. And he was glad to do it. They all signed it."

Clinton was not the only president to sign the picture. When President George W. Bush later visited Eglin, Dari decided to get his signature as well.

After a short speech, Bush came to the front of the stage and reached down to shake hands with the crowd. In the crush of people to get near Bush, Dari got the signature and then pointed to Joseph's mother, Bridget, who was stuck further back in the dense crowd.

Bush took direct action.

"He started leaning over the rope line," Dari recalled. "The secret service had his belt loop, and were holding on to him, and he reaches out and he grabs Bridget's shirt material and yanks her through the crowd to the front."

The Wounds That Do Not Heal

In addition to those whose loved ones died in the attack, there were those families faced with tragic wounds and changes in the survivors. The following account is not the only one of the pain of dealing with a wounded survivor. It is presented here as one of many similar situations.

The son of one of the victims, who asked that his name be withheld, was just six years old when an explosion he never saw nor heard nevertheless shattered his life. Years later he followed in the footsteps of his father's career, joining the Air Force Reserves.

Long after the attack, he still remembers how it altered "not only my father's life, but the lives of myself and family would be adversely changed forever."

As a six year old "sleeping safely in bed each night under the blanket of freedom and protection his father would ultimately sacrifice everything for," he wrote:

Through the Perilous Night

"I should have been concerned about G.I Joe storming the beaches of my sandbox, or if my mother had properly removed the crust of my peanut butter and jelly sandwich. Instead, my adolescent thoughts were consumed with if my father would wake up the next morning, how can I be the man of the house, why did my accidental slamming the pantry door cause my dad to curl into a ball on the floor and start crying? These thoughts are the ones that would saturate my mind, my dreams, and my play as I grew older.

I remember when the bombing happened. I did not exactly understand why my mother was so upset or concerned. She did an amazing job of sheltering my sister and me from the news coverage. I remember speaking with my father on the phone and knowing he was okay. When he arrived home from his deployment, after the attack, he had the usual gifts and trinkets that a military child is accustomed to. My sister and I received matching stuffed camels that we were extremely excited about. Over the next few weeks my action figures would go on adventure after adventure with their faithful companion that travels across the oceans to join in.

I remember that my father would complain of severe headaches and blurred vision when we would be watching our favorite television shows or playing *The Lion King* on his Sega Genesis handheld together. My sister and I would bring the handheld game system to the emergency room when the headaches became unbearable for him. It was our distraction and reprieve from the very adult world we were going to be so abruptly thrown into.

I remember the night my world would no longer be defined by chasing the ice cream truck down the drive with my father laughing close behind. I came in from slaying the evil Sith ruler Darth Vader, which greatly resembled the post of our carport in base housing. I noticed my father laying on the couch, cool rag over his eyes, our dog enthusiastically greeting me at the door, and my mother in the kitchen cleaning the dishes from dinner. She motioned for me to be quiet and informed me that he had another headache.

I had become accustomed to the routine over the previous weeks and began quietly putting my toys away for bedtime. As I went about my routine I saw my father get off the sofa and stagger toward the bathroom located on the first floor in the entrance hallway. I had never seen him walk that way before and felt something was very wrong...

He began to projectile vomit and fell onto the floor. He was laying lifeless in his own excrement. My mother rushed to him and instructed my sister and I to stay back. She called the emergency services and we were explicitly told to take Maggie to the bathroom upstairs, shut the door, and wait there until she came to get us. She was attempting to preserve our innocence, to ensure our childhood would not be plagued with these memories and thoughts.

As my sister and I waited in the bathroom I could hear what can only be described as anguish and commotion down the stairs. This was only being amplified by my sister who was mortified, crying as though our dad was already deceased.

There was a small bathroom window that overlooked the driveway, front yard, and street. We heard the sirens as the ambulance approached the house and saw the flashing of red lights coming through the small window. I stood on the tips of my toes on the upper portion of the toilet making every effort to gather any shred of evidence that my sister was not correct...

As I peered through our only opening to the reality that would be our new lives I saw the stretcher coming out. Men working on my father, and them loading him to the ambulance. As they pulled out of sight I managed to find my way from the top of the toilet to the floor, leaning against the wall, flabbergasted and stunned. I remember having some tears but throughout the process I remember being the stronger one. Whether that be for myself or my sister I am not certain to this day.

The next weeks were filled with uncertainty, tears, and wondering. At six years old I would no longer be a child. At six years old I would be a man, who only had a very short time with his father to learn the lessons of life that should be passed on. My time would consist of being in a hospital waiting room wondering if my father was ever going to wake up, or in the room with him.

Watching machines breathe for him, monitor him, and asking anyone who walked into the room what they were doing to help my father.

The hospital began to feel more normal than home did. Home was riddled with flashbacks of seeing my father fall in the hallway. Remembering the lights flashing through the window. The hospital was where he was going to get better and I wanted to be there when he would finally wake up.

When the day came that he regained consciousness the man lying in the bed in front of me was not my father. He did not recognize me, my name was as foreign to him as my understanding of the situation. I saw my mother in tears as the doctors reassured her that this would all be temporary and she attempted to emulate their false sense of security for my sister and I.

There were words and phrases that I would quickly become entirely too familiar with. My mother would eloquently put things like stroke, traumatic brain injury, or short-term memory loss into the vernacular of a six and seven-year-old. As we began to understand ... my father began to remember. He once more knew who I was. He could tell me he loved me if only by the look in his eyes and he still struggles to find the words. Things were going to be normal again! I was sure of it. I was naively unaware of the long term repercussions this event would have on me...

[But] the time in the hospital was far from over for my father, as well. Physical therapy, speech therapy, cognitive rehabilitation. The simple, everyday task of pouring a glass of water or tying his shoes was impossible. I took it upon myself to be there for him. I was going to go through every painful step with the man that I saw in front of me. I knew the one I called Dad was buried deep within the broken shell of the person that now held his place. I was determined to pull him out and bring him home.

My innocence to the harsh realities of life would dwindle as quickly as I grew older by the day. I saw my father struggling, incensed with the inability to do the task he could once do, recall the information he was just asked to repeat, or simply form words into a coherent sentence. Fair was no longer a concept that I had the luxury to believe in. It became abundantly apparent, to even a six-year-old, that the world was full of evil people and it took good men to fight for those who could not fight for themselves. I knew that my father was one of those men. I sat beaming with pride during his decoration ceremony when he received his Purple Heart.

I learned how to fight for myself and the ones I loved as I stood by him as he relearned to throw a ball with his son or rollerblade in the driveway. I spent countless hours working through speech therapy with him as the therapist recognized his more positive outlook when I was in attendance. He would put in a 100% effort to not let me walk away disappointed from his session, showing me that progress was being made. He fought tirelessly to be the man I remembered. I watched him fight until the fight in him slowly faded as though a candle that flickered out.

He had reached the threshold. He had recovered as much as humanly possible. He would never be able to return to a job. Never be able to drive again. His new normal would never be good enough for himself.

It is all too common in the medical community to see a diagnosis that says 'secondary to.' My father was suffering from depression secondary to traumatic brain injury. He knew in his soul that he would never fully be the man he was. He feared that it would never be good enough for my mother, sister, or myself.

Nonetheless he feared he would never be good enough for himself. All the effort and fight in the world could not erase the damage that had been done. His new reality was our new normal.

We all suffered as he suffered from post-traumatic stress disorder. My father's reclusive habits did not only isolate himself but my family as well.

We could not go to public places with large crowds due to his fear of a terrorist attack. Loud noises would cause him to become increasingly agitated until he snapped at the person who was causing it. A car backfiring would inevitably find him in the fetal position, tears welling in his eyes, and rocking back and forth.

The devastation of the traumatic brain injury causing his stroke was only the tip of a much larger chaos that would be in our lives. The Khobar Tower bombing did not only cause an explosion 7676.4 miles overseas but it would cause an un-fillable crater in my and my families lives.

I understand that the man I now hug is not the same man that once held me as a child. Through adversity our relationship has grown. These experiences have molded me into the man I am today. I will never know what life could have been. I will never be able to purge the traumatic memories of watching my father die and another man re-emerge in his likeness."

His pride in his father is undiminished by suffering and time.

"My father is a good man who stood at the door and said, 'you will not enter here.' My father defended the innocence of my youth with his life. It is with great misfortune that very innocence was stolen from me prematurely. I have since taken up the mantle - following in his example, standing against evil.

His grandchildren will hear on a daily basis that their 'Papa' is a hero. I will ensure they are his constant reminder that his sacrifice was not in vain. Although my innocence was shattered like the glass in his dormitory, his grandson's will remain solid and whole.

I will never see the man I once called "Dad" again. He is long gone and my memories of him are few and foggy. I will, however, always hold dear the lessons taught to me from the man I have come to love and cherish even more. Perseverance, dedication, love, humility, and forgiveness. These are the things that cannot be taken by a bomb."

***

These examples are just a few samples of the river of grief suffered by the survivors' family members. There are many more.

"The Peoples Promise"

Immediately after the bombing, families of the casualties wrote Rep. Joe Scarborough (R-FL) asking that Congress officially recognize the sacrifice. Three months later, Congress passed a concurrent resolution honoring the victims who "exemplified all that is best and most virtuous in the American people."[20]

---

[20] Appendix A: Text of 1996 US House Resolution HR200

For some, the last words of the resolution carried an important pledge. It affirmed that Congress "assures the members of the Armed Forces serving anywhere in the world that their well-being and interest will at all times be given the highest priority." Some have referred to this resolution as "The People's Promise."

That well-being became a priority for someone who had only fleetingly known one of the victims. Years later, a high school classmate of Joseph Rimkus, Beth Salyers, found herself guided into a vocation to fulfill the promise to protect the nation's protectors.

> "I didn't know the circumstances of his death would be the case study for which I learned force protection design as an Air Force Engineer," Salyers recalled. "I didn't know that just five years after his death, I would be deployed to the same operation in Saudi Arabia, safer because of the lessons learned from his sacrifice. Or that I'd spend every morning of that 90-day deployment visiting his memorial there grateful for having known him.
>
> The circumstances of my life and my career have made it impossible to forget Joseph. I'm so grateful for that. The pain, the loss of a friend, of my naivety and innocence, was not for nothing. I gained life, knowledge, awareness, and gratitude. I'm indebted to Joseph and those, like him, who died defending our nation and those of us in it. We didn't know then, but we know now."

Joseph Rimkus' Basic Training graduation photo bearing prominent signatures including: Col. Doug Cochran, two U.S. Presidents, a U.S. Senator, U.S. Congressmen, U.S. Military Generals, Joseph's Commanders and many friends.

CHAPTER 7
Homes of the Brave

Two days after the bombing William Schooley returned to Kirtland AFB and his wife Missy. Three years later, in 1999, he was medically retired from the Air Force after serving 15 years as a Munitions Systems Specialist.

After retiring, Schooley co-founded the Khobar Towers Bombing Survivors Association and serves as its president. The association's goal is to ensure Khobar Towers "Never Be Forgotten." He has appeared on Fox News, BBC World Wide Radio and in numerous articles.

In 2006, as Schooley puts it, he "was blessed with a son" and is a stay-at-home Dad. He is a Freemason and a Shriner.

"I left Khobar Towers two days after the bombing, it was still on TV when I got home. A few days later I was back at work, and two guys from Supply came to see me. Both Vietnam Combat Vets, one was Army and the other was a Marine. My boss came and told me John and Gill are here to see you, they are outside.

I go to meet them, and I mean these are two big tough dudes, they both come over and give me a hug and say 'we understand.' We talked for a couple of minutes and they left. I had no idea what had just happened. For the next couple of years they would show up ask me how I was doing chat for a couple of minutes and leave. It was a dark time for me, I didn't ever thank them or give it much thought. But later I realized they had taught me what the Brotherhood of Vets is all about, you take care of your own and never leave a man behind even if it is back in the States. Vietnam Vets often say, 'If you weren't there you don't understand.' Gill and John understood."

***

In 1997, Security Policeman Larry Oliver left active duty and served as a Guardsman with units in Connecticut, Utah and Wisconsin, primarily one weekend a month and occasionally longer two-week periods.

After the September 2001 attacks, Oliver and other Guardsmen were activated to fill positions at Langley Air Force Base in Virginia. He married in 2002, deployed to Cyprus that summer and eventually retired from the Guard in August of 2017.

As of this writing Oliver has started college and is studying to be a medical assistant. "I was getting bored too quickly," he explained.

After careers as an electrician and a security policeman, Oliver chose the medical field because he felt it was "more constructive."

"It goes back to that desire to help people," he said.

***

John Gaydos left the Air Force in 1997, following a medical board.

> "My wife tells me that I am not the same man that left to go to Saudi. I know that she is right and I have made many journal notes where I recognize that when I left to go to Khobar I was a 25-year-old with my whole life ahead of me. I was in peak physical shape and could achieve any goal I set in my life. As it turns out my goal would be survival…
>
> Somewhere along the way it dawned on me that what was happening was no different than my childhood. Like a teenager who rebels because they

are trying to establish an identity, I was rebelling trying to establish the new me.

I eventually quit trying to hold onto my old life and recognized, that life was over. I even had a personal funeral for my former self. I established June 25th, as my new birthday, the day I came into this world. If you can't change the past look for the positive. Instead of trying to fix myself to continue with my former goals I developed new goals and aspirations. I made sure that I was realistic and only set goals that I can achieve with the body and mind I have today. If you have PTSD you know what I mean.

Today my wife says I smile more and she notices the difference in me. I am more outgoing than I have been in years and in some ways I would even say more so than I was when I left to go to Khobar.

If there is one wish I could have granted to me today it would be to get to meet the guys that set that bomb off. Twenty years ago I might have done something very violent to them, today I would take them with me through the course of my day and let them see that what they tried to destroy has come back to be a positive that allows me to have a positive influence on those around me. I have many friends that I otherwise would never have met and I have helped them even as they have helped me. Instead of breaking my Christian beliefs they have become stronger than ever before. Instead of making me afraid of terrorism it makes me want to stand and confront it in any way that I can.

Lastly I would thank them for taking a young man that was living in the world but not really stopping to understand and appreciate the gift of life and making me into a man that seeks out the meaning of why I am here and gives thanks daily for the life I have."

***

After returning to Pope, Trena Schmidt deployed again in 1997 to Kuwait and Germany. In September of 1999, she moved to Kirtland AFB, New Mexico. In December of 2000, she married Michael Schmidt, a fellow airman she had met at Pope. In February of 2005, she was assigned to Ellsworth Air Force Base near Rapid City, South Dakota.

After 22 years on active duty, Schmidt retired from the Air Force in July of 2009, and started civil service work for the Air Force. She and Michael have two 14-year-old girl twins. In her free time, she likes to birdwatch, camp, fish and watch college football and NASCAR.

***

After 23 years of service, Leighton Reid "dropped his retirement papers" when he returned to the States several months following the attack. He later returned to Saudi Arabia, but this time with his wife Anne, working an additional six years as a Disaster Preparedness Advisor to the Royal Saudi Air Force back at King Abdul Aziz Air Base (Dhahran) and then in Riyadh. Reid was obligated to finish his contract with the Saudis for an additional 15 months following the 9-11 attack after first evacuating his wife and dog. He followed his gut feelings and departed the Kingdom just five months before his Riyadh compound was attacked in 2003.

Upon repatriation to the States, Reid worked as an Emergency Management defense contractor in Panama City and currently at MacDill AFB in Tampa, Florida.

Along with Emergency Management planning, Reid regularly instructs Air Force personnel on Chemical, Biological, Radiological, and Nuclear survival skills with an emphasis on conventional attack measures learned first-hand at Khobar. Two of the Reid's three children have or are currently serving in the Air Force, with the third child working in law enforcement. He plans to retire in the next few years and "enjoy the sunsets."

***

Selena Zuhoski, the paralegal, retired from the Air Force in 2006 as a Master Sergeant and settled in Maryland. After retiring, she worked as a paralegal for the Department of Justice in a cybercrime unit until 2018. She is married and raised two children. She has two grandchildren.

> "As time passed it became clear that even though the rest of the world had moved on, I was still reliving the moments during and after the blast," she said. "It became harder and harder to sleep, eat and work. I always felt anxious and distracted.
>
> It reached a point where I had to seek help, looking for an explanation for my feelings.
>
> After a number of emotionally painful visits to various military doctors and mental health experts, it was determined that I was suffering from PTSD (Post Traumatic Stress Disorder). To this day, especially on the anniversary of the bombing, I find myself feeling anxious and depressed.
>
> The support of my loving family helps me through these tough times. Additionally, the TBI from the blast led to a diagnosis of permanent brain damage that causes me to have seizures. These are

controlled by medication that I will have to take for the rest of my life.

Even with all of that, I am proud to have served this country and would do it over again if asked. I also try to stay connected with other Khobar survivors through social media contact and assist in organizing an annual wreath laying ceremony at Arlington."

As with many of the survivors, she is upbeat in spite of the ordeal.

"I taught myself how to paint watching YouTube videos, I volunteer at my local Humane Society, set painting and prop making for a local community theater group, and I'm learning to play ukulele."

***

Mike Dunn left the Air Force in late January of 1997. He moved close to his daughter, his one goal being "to be in that baby's life."

He started working for a paging company in Cleveland. Over the years he was promoted and moved up in different companies. In November of 1997, he married a high school sweetheart, Tracy. They have a son and a daughter and are still "very happily married."

***

Scott Wolff retired from the Air Force in 2002 as a Master Sergeant (E7). He is married with four stepchildren and lives in South Carolina near Shaw Air Force Base.

Wolff now works for Caterpillar as a Computer Numerically Controlled Specialist, working with any machinery that uses computer systems to control the operations.

Wolff's memory of the bombing remains vivid.

"Twenty-two years later, every time someone asks me or I tell someone about the details of the night of the bombing, I'm overcome with emotion, sometimes having to stop to gather myself and choke back tears. I believe I do have some PTSD from the experience but have not sought counseling for it."

***

Several months after returning to the states, Michael Willis suffered an aneurysm. This left him with issues to deal with on top of the post-traumatic stress brought on by the attack.

"The struggle is what's PTSD and what's memory loss."

As time went by, Willis continued to be disappointed to find that so few people knew about the attack.

"The biggest thing that stuck out to me was the feeling that nobody knows, nobody cares, nobody remembers who we are. Even fellow airmen seemed ignorant of the attack. It hurts."

Willis left the Air Force in 2001 because "I got tired of deploying" and transferred to the Air Force Reserve, where he serves in the cyber defense career field and reached the rank of Senior Master Sergeant (E8). He now works as a project manager for Cisco Systems. He has three children, one of whom recently married.

"Through all of this was my wife, Shelly. She was and is my reason for living.

Unfortunately Khobar Towers was not my only brush with death. Just four months after returning home I had a severe headache during M-16 refresher training. I waited until late that night to ask my pregnant wife to take me to the emergency room at Langley Air Force Base. After a CAT scan I was transferred to Portsmouth Naval Hospital where I was diagnosed with a ruptured venous malformation, similar to a brain aneurism. The doctor said that at best I should be a vegetable, if not dead. Obviously God wasn't done with me.

Just a few weeks before this latest brush with death, we had been told that my wife had miscarried our first child. The doctor in the Emergency Room kept saying, 'it looks like the pregnancy aborted.' I lost count of the number of times he said the word, 'abort.' I finally asked him to find another word to use as it obviously just increased our distress in the situation.

About a week after that we learned that my wife did not lose the baby but it still could happen. I believe I had a more difficult time dealing with this than my near-death experiences.

Just a little over a year ago on the anniversary of the bombing I broke down and finally admitted that I was still living the events of that night over and over again. I didn't want to admit I had Post Traumatic Stress Disorder (PTSD). I saw myself as a mentally and emotionally strong man and PTSD is a sign of weakness, or so I thought. I now understand the truth.

PTSD has nothing to do with toughness or manliness ... I have good days and I have bad days as I struggle to deal with it."

In addition to work and family, Willis teaches a class, "Reboot – Combat Recovery," to victim of trauma and their families.

"It helps me to recover as well.

There have been ups and downs over the years, I have faith in God. Everything happens for a reason.

All we can do is live our lives to honor those who didn't survive."

***

For Doug Cochran, history had a pleasant surprise.

"Ironically enough ... our son David is in the 58th Fighter Squadron ... and is scheduled to take command in June of 2019."

***

Jessica Bradshaw admits, as did many others, to survivor guilt:

"Why did I survive? I should have been dead."

When she had gone back to her dorm the day after the attack—

"My door was actually on my bed. If I had been in bed, the door would have just nailed me. The sliding glass door that I had been trying to close moments before the bomb went off had been embedded into the opposite wall."

For a time, loud noises would make her jump, and she could not watch movies with people covered in blood. However:

"I'm really good now."

Bradshaw left the Air Force in February of 1997. She followed a friend to Washington State and served in the Air National Guard until 2003.

She married Mike Bradshaw, a DoD employee in an intelligence squadron, in 2008.

"He was the first person I told the entire story to."

They have one seven-year-old daughter. Bradshaw earned a master's degree in Social Work in 2007. She has been Sexual Assault Response Coordinator for Fairchild AFB near Spokane, Washington since 2010.

***

Dusty Huntley spent the next two to three years "going to bed every night just to be jolted awake within the first five minutes, but it finally subsided.

> "I thought I had wrecked my career during a deployment in Afghanistan when I yelled at our team leader, a lieutenant colonel. I didn't realize it at the time, but he arranged it for me and my airmen to return home earlier than we expected. I guess, he figured it out before I did, that I was still dealing with effects of the Khobar Towers attack.
>
> I made an appointment with mental health after realizing I had a problem when I again blew up at my supervisor back at Grand Forks. It was probably the hardest appointment I ever had. I went through several sessions with her over a six- to nine-month period when she diagnosed me with PTSD."

Huntley retired in 2010 as a Master Sergeant.

"It still happens: the jolted wakeups. It's not an everyday occurrence, but the memories are still there 20 years later.

I tried therapy through the Veterans Administration (VA), but they didn't seem to care. I tried other things, painting, puzzles, video games. One day, my wife asked if I wanted to get a tattoo and it turns out it was the best thing I did. The artist was a military dependent and could relate, and the pain from the needles seemed to ease the mental pain.

So, I found solace in getting tattoos and paying tribute to our fallen Airmen.

I can remember that night like it was yesterday, but for whatever reason everything in between seems to fade away over time. A smell, a scene, picture, thought or even just a casual mention of that day can just make me cry thinking of those people we lost and all of those that were filling the triage area with their blood and wounds. No, nothing will let me forget that day..."

***

Angel Marsh's career in the Air Force ended up including duty in England, Al Kharj, Saudi Arabia, Okinawa, Nebraska, Iraq, Virginia, Qatar and Delaware. She retired in 2015 and moved back to Louisiana.

Marsh's memories aren't all she has from Khobar. In 1999, she married Christopher Marsh. Christopher is the airman who carried her outside when she was injured. They have three children.

***

With all that so many of the survivors suffered, many have nevertheless moved on with their lives. They often look back at the trauma as something that has forged them into who they are today.

As Jessica Bradshaw put it:

"It sounds crazy – I wouldn't ever want to go through Khobar Towers again, but at the same time, I wouldn't give up that experience – It has become a part of who I am."

Appendix A

Chairman's Mark for H. Con Res. 200

Concurrent Resolution

Honoring the victims of the June 25, 1996 terrorist bombing in Dhahran, Saudi Arabia.

Whereas on June 25, 1996, a terrorist truck bomb struck a military housing compound in Dhahran, Saudi Arabia and killed 19 members of the Armed Forces and wounded hundreds of others;

Whereas the members of the Armed Forces killed and wounded in the bombing were defending the national security interest of the United States;

Whereas the defense of the United States national interest continues to require deployment of members of the Armed Forces to other countries;

Whereas the members of the Armed Forces are called upon to perform duties that place their lives at risk from terrorist elements hostile to the United States;

Whereas global terrorism has demonstrated no respect for the historic rules of war, no reluctance to strike against innocent and defenseless individuals, and a willingness to engage in tactics against which conventional defenses are difficult;

Whereas it is the duty of the President and the military chain of command to take steps necessary to keep members of the Armed Forces protected and as safe as the nature of their mission permits;

Whereas the people of the United States stand with those who have volunteered to serve their country and grieve at the loss of those who to quote Lincoln, "have given their last full measure of devotion" to the security and well-being of the United States;

Whereas the members of the Armed Forces serving in Saudi Arabia and around the world demonstrate valor and a faith in the American way of life that reflects honorably not only on themselves but upon the country they represent;

Whereas the military personnel who lost their lives on June 25, 1996, in the bombing in Dhahran died in the honorable service of their Nation and exemplified all that is best and most virtuous in the American people: Now, therefore, be it

Resolved by the House of Representatives (the Senate concurring), that Congress hereby-

(1) recognizes the 19 members of the Armed Forces who died in the terrorist truck bombing in Dhahran, Saudi Arabia, on June 25, 1996, and honors them for their service and sacrifice;

(2) Calls upon the Nation to hold fast the memory of those who died;

(3) Extends its sympathies to the families of those who died; and

(4) Assures the members of the Armed Forces serving anywhere in the world that their well-being and interest will at all times be given the highest priority.

ABOUT THE COVER

The cover of ***Through the Perilous Night*** combines artistry and symbolism through the work of two professionals.

Jim Lamb of Jim Lamb Photography combined a Department of Defense photo* with his own photo of a grieving airman to portray the attack in symbolic terms.

Jim is a retired Air Force Veteran living in Colorado Springs, Colorado.

Professional graphic artist Bruce Gardner then produced a cover design pulling the elements into a vivid, striking image that "our flag was still there."

Bruce has been a graphic artist for 40 years, including work at Fawcette Technical Publications, 1105 Media, The Kansas City Star, San Francisco Giants, and as a freelance designer/illustrator. Samples of his work can be found at www.rbgardner.com

Our hats off to Jim and Bruce for a stirring tribute.

* *The appearance of the U.S. Department of Defense (DoD) visual information does not imply or constitute DoD endorsement.*

ABOUT THE AUTHOR
Paul Sherbo

Photo by Randy Snyder, Captain USN (Ret.)

Paul Sherbo served in the Navy and Navy Reserve for 30 years, retiring as a Captain in 2006.

His book, *Unsinkable Sailors: The fall and rise of the last crew of USS Frank E. Evans*, is an account of the June 1969 collision of *Evans* with an aircraft carrier, HMAS *Melbourne.*

Fish Out of Water is Paul's second book describing the Iraq Campaign as he lived it during his service there. Paul has also written stories for a number of newspapers and magazines.

Paul and his wife, Diana Carlson-Sherbo, live in Colorado and have three children.

Visit Paul's website at www.paulsherbo.com

Additional Patriot Media, Incorporated Books

All titles are listed by author's name and may be purchased at: **www.patriotmediainc.com** & **www.amazon.com,** with most selections available for Kindle Readers. For book reviews and descriptions visit our website: **www.patriotmediainc.com**.

Paul Sherbo

Unsinkable Sailors: The fall and rise of the last crew of USS Frank E. Evans

Fish Out of Water

Submarine Adventures From D.M. Ulmer

Silent Battleground

Beyond Silent Battleground

Shadows of Heroes

The Cold War Beneath

Ensure Plausible Deniability

Skagerrak

Shared Glory

Additional titles by D.M. Ulmer

Missing Person

The Roche Harbor Caper

The Long Beach Caper

Count the Ways

Where or When

Brett Kneisley
DVD-Tour of USS Clamagore
Starring D.M. Ulmer as the tour guide

Robert & Billie Nicholson
Pearl Harbor Honor Flight: One Last Goodbye

Nelson O. Ottenhausen
Civil War II
The Blue Heron
The Killing Zone
The Sin Slayer
Jugs & Bottles
The Naked Warrior
Little Hawk & Lobo
Shadow Wolves
Black Mist of the Trinity

Art Giberson
The Mighty O

B.K. Bryans
Those '67 Blues
Flight to Redemption
The Dog Robbers
Arizona Grit
Brannigan Rides Again

Joseph C. Engel
Flight of the Silver Eagle

Peter Clark
Staff Monkeys: A Stockbrokers Journey through the Global War on Terror

Troy Montes
Grampa Joe: Portrait of a Quiet Hero

Hal Olsen
Up An' Atom

Roger Chaney
Carquinez Straits

Paul Stuligross
The Donkey

Jack Verneski
Scarecrow Season

Ralph McDougal
A Cowboy Goes to War
Mules to Missiles

Chris Schultz
Lincoln's Treasure

Dari Bradley
Hickory Nuts in the Driveway

Hannah Ackerman
I Kept My Chin Up

www.ingramcontent.com/pod-product-compliance
Lightning Source LLC
Chambersburg PA
CBHW071716090426
42738CB00009B/1790